STEPHEN DEPONEO

TAXI FOR
KIEV

THE STORY OF SIX STRANGERS, CROSSING SIX BORDERS, OVER SIX DAYS

First published by Pitch Publishing, 2022

Pitch Publishing
A2 Yeoman Gate
Yeoman Way
Worthing
Sussex
BN13 3QZ
www.pitchpublishing.co.uk
info@pitchpublishing.co.uk

A CIP catalogue record is available for this book
from the British Library.

ISBN 978 1 80150 113 2

Typesetting and origination by Pitch Publishing
Printed and bound in Great Britain by TJ Books, Padstow

Contents

For Barb

The saying goes, 'Don't regret what you do in life, only regret what you don't.'

My big regret in writing this book is that I didn't do it sooner, when Barb was still with us. Mum loved to read.

RIP DEAR MOTHER

Introduction

ONE OF the reasons I have written this book is simply because people close to me for many years have suggested that I put pen to paper. On more than one occasion I have had the material, but it's just been a case of never actually getting around to writing it down. 'Never regret what you do in life, only regret what you don't,' as the saying goes. Therefore, I thought, after so many trips I'd finally give it a go. Primarily this book is about a unique and truly amazing adventure of six boys, all strangers, who met up at a local boozer and then embarked on a trip of a lifetime into the great unknown.

There will be times in this book where I will digress slightly and go off on small tangents. You see, it was inevitable that certain episodes from this mystery tour would unlock memories from bygone trips. If I can open doors hidden deep away in my memory bank as I progress with my writing, remembering experiences that are linked, then I feel I owe it to myself to put them on paper, for my own benefit really but if you enjoy your perusal then all the better.

Another reason to try and record the experiences from this trip is the fact that, having had the great fortune to have been on so many excursions over the years, unfortunately most of them are now a blur. Time does things like that to your memory; at least now I will have something to look back on.

Stories of real adventures, of previous escapades in bygone days in far-off lands, running around Europe with the boys. Life back in the late 1970s and into the 80s really was one long adventure; it was for me anyway. Those days are now distant memories, albeit blurred, that I will take to my grave.

I know for a fact that there are hundreds if not thousands of boys and girls who have travelled more often and much further afield than I have over the decades, following our beloved Liverpool Football Club around.

People have had far greater and more dramatic times than I could ever imagine, but to date I have been on more than 50 European away trips.

I could never claim to be the biggest or best Liverpool supporter ever to have lived but I truly do count my blessings on my score. How many can say they have had even one experience under their belt? At the risk of boring you, I will list the places I've visited. As I mentioned earlier it's more for my sake than yours, so feel free to skip.

This is my perfect opportunity to log some of my great adventures. This list is of European away fixtures only, presented in no particular order:

Olympic Stadium: Athens, Greece
Emirates Stadium: London, England

Amsterdam Arena: Amsterdam, Netherlands
Camp Nou: Barcelona, Spain
St Jacob-Park: Basel, Switzerland

Stadion Balgarska Armia: Sofia, Bulgaria
Parkhead: Glasgow, Scotland
Westfalenstadion: Dortmund, Germany
Philips Stadion: Eindhoven, Holland
Heysel Stadium: Brussels, Belgium
Olimpiyskiy National Sports Complex: Kyiv, Ukraine

Stadion Miejski im. Henryka Reymana: Kraków, Poland
Stadion u Nisy: Liberec, Czech Rep
Stade Louis II: Monaco, France
Stade Vélodrome: Marseille, France
Olympic Stadium: Munich, Germany
Allianz Arena: Munich, Germany
Santiago Bernabéu Stadium: Madrid, Spain
Stadio San Paolo: Naples, Italy
Estádio das Antas: Porto, Portugal
Parc des Princes: Paris, France
Stadio Olimpico: Roma, Italy
Estadio Benito Villamarín: Betis, Spain
San Siro: Milan, Italy
Wembley: London, England
Wanda Metropolitano: Madrid, Spain
Vodafone Stadium: Istanbul, Turkey

I have been to some of these stadia on more than one occasion, so I am quite proud of that little stat. It's not the highest count of all but I'm chuffed to bits, proud and honoured. It has been an absolute privilege to have had so many experiences you couldn't possibly buy. You may have noticed one serious omission from my list: Istanbul. This little event in ours club's wonderful history was, can you believe, missed by yours truly.

My wife Donna and I were building a business together over on the east coast of England by May 2005 and were very close to opening our establishment. We overshot our rebuild budget slightly and in fact had to sell the family car in order to get open in time for the May bank holidays. We even had tickets for the Champions League Final but unfortunately needs must and we had no option but to get our priorities in order.

The pain of missing out on that wonderful night in Turkey will never leave us, but I can justifiably say that the sacrifice paid off in as much as our business was a huge success. Donna and I enjoyed a quality way of life, running a very successful business for almost eight years. We enjoyed our stay in Lincolnshire very much but decided we had reached a time in our lives where we needed to return home. The main reason was because our little troop of grandchildren was starting to appear at a rapid rate. We both hated the thought of missing out on watching them grow up. Donna will tell you that I beat myself up far too much when I say I am eager to make up for lost time with them. At the time of writing we have eight, with another one on the way. It sounds a lot but with five children the chances were always in favour of reaching double figures.

Another reason for returning home was that although we did manage to get to a few European away trips while living on the east coast, being away from our place of worship was starting to weigh heavy!

I have been so lucky in life to have experienced many book-worthy trips but have never managed to write them all down before, although I have often contemplated it. This is my account of just one trip – a momentous road trip across western Europe, far behind the old Iron Curtain, in an eight-seater taxi.

* * *

In this book I make reference to Scousers this and Scousers that! In saying this from time to time, I am making only a regional reference. Okay, Scousers are a different breed and have certain traits others don't possess but in the main, these boys and girls can be found in any city across England and beyond. In reality, underneath it all, the main difference is the accent.

1

The Planning

THE WEEK building up to the 2018 final of the greatest competition in European club football was one of real mixed emotions for Donna and I, plus thousands and thousands of other Redmen. The want and the need to be there in Kyiv was at times overwhelming. There were stories aplenty of family, friends and colleagues booking trips left, right and centre and this only served to make the quest to be there even more desperate.

We had spent countless hours on many different websites trying to find a reasonably priced excursion to the Ukrainian capital. Hopes were raised and then dashed on numerous occasions; one minute excited that we could get there and the next disappointed because of places being filled up at an alarmingly rapid pace and also because of the spiralling costs involved. We had stayed up into the wee small hours of the Wednesday morning prior to the game, researching avenues that could possibly get us on the move to yet another European Cup Final. The event is better known as the

Champions League Final these days, although locally this enormous cup is known as 'Old Big Ears'. It always has been and always will be.

Our planning may have been a little late and a bit too close to the day of the game itself to expect flights to still be available, but as the big day drew closer and closer the desire to be there in Kyiv was becoming all-consuming. The fact that two of the city's most collectable items had landed at our feet had made our research even more desperate. A source that will forever remain anonymous had offered me two tickets for the final, all above board I must add and at face value, absolutely no touting involved here. Just an amazing act of thoughtfulness that will be appreciated forever. Sir, I owe you a debt of gratitude! The value of the two tickets I had been offered was €280, and these were nowhere near the top-price seats on sale.

The whole football circus is designed to fleece. Tourists will undoubtedly pay the going rate and locals feel a duty/need to be there. This not only maintains demand but increases it to astronomical levels. Liverpool Football Club turn away on average 20,000 unsuccessful ticket applications for every home league match. I rest my case!

Many years ago, after getting stung once by a ticket tout, it was there and then that I promised myself never again to allow myself to be ripped off by these people. In 1976 and only a month before my 15th birthday I had gone down to Wembley by coach with my elder brother Paul. With no match ticket in my pocket for the Charity Shield against Southampton, just before kick-off I found myself with no alternative but to pay one of the Cockney spiv arseholes £18. That was triple the face-value cost, gobshite! I've never had a ticket off a tout since and nor will I ever again. I'd rather miss the game than line the pockets of an entrepreneur with few morals.

Back to 2018 and after hours and hours of trawling the internet, it was with huge disappointment that we resigned ourselves to not being able to make it this time. I don't think either of us slept well that night, constantly going over and over in our minds the options, if any, that were possible. The missed opportunity was starting to sting already. My overriding thoughts were that as the big day drew closer the desire and the agony of missing out would become almost unbearable, especially after not being in Istanbul; we will never get over that one!

I was still in the same frame of mind when we were driving to work the following day. It was the Wednesday morning, four days before the big game itself. During our commute, Donna made a phone call to someone unknown to me, and after she had finished she turned to me and said, 'Okay, you're going tonight – by taxi.' 'WHAT?' I exclaimed, astonished by her words. 'One of the lads from work had texted me the details of a taxi firm that were running a trip,' she said calmly.

My head was spinning; this was all happening so fast and before I could gather my thoughts and respond Donna continued, 'You're going to have to finish work early today, go home, pack and be back at Anfield by 6pm tonight!' What a girl.

My head was all over the place. My emotions were going into overdrive; excitement, sadness, happiness, disappointment, selfishness, in fact almost every emotion you could think of was racing through my head. I was really uneasy about it all as Donna had gone to all this trouble to enable me to go on this huge road trip alone. She was sacrificing one of her own ambitions but was determined to make sure that I got to go.

Donna knew only too well that the last option of travelling was to be on my own, or without her at least. This was the only option that was on the table as time was running out fast, albeit it was not my preferred choice I must add. I know Donna wasn't too comfortable with this mode of transport for a couple of reasons. Firstly, she doesn't travel too well; she tends to get car sick unless she is sat up front or driving. The poor girl even gets seasick on the Mersey Ferry.

Sadly, the real reason for Donna not wanting to do a road trip of this huge proportion was the heartbreaking fact that when she was a five-year-old girl and the apple of her father Maurice Robinson's eye, Donna and her family were to experience the most tragic of all tragic events, which would change people's lives forever, and not in a good way.

Maurice was in a top Liverpool band that went by the name of The Hoedowners. They were hugely successful in the 1960s and bookings were coming in from near and far. One such booking ultimately turned out to be their last gig and heartbreakingly proved fatal.

The Hoedowners were on a mammoth road trip themselves, heading to Turkey to entertain the troops stationed overseas. After such a long and arduous trip, the band were involved in a major road traffic accident only one hour away from their destination. Maurice and two other members of the band tragically died at the scene. The lead singer was a young lady named Prudence White, who was on her very first trip with the band; she lost her life on her debut tour at 21 years old.

The indie band Viola Beach's accident in Sweden in 2016 was strikingly similar and a very loud echo of the heartache Donna and her family had suffered back in 1970. That heartache never truly leaves you. Time may fade and dilute things a little but these momentous, life-changing experiences can never go away. Just how does a five-year-old girl who idolised her daddy ever get over something like that? I sincerely doubt she ever has, to tell you the truth, or that she ever will, not fully. How could she?

Donna has had a massive void in her life for almost 50 years. No matter how many other family members and friends have attempted to fill it, that void has never gone away. Mo is never forgotten within the circles of the family and even further afield within the city of Liverpool. He is remembered and mentioned at all family gatherings.

As I said, 'What a girl!'

The rest of the morning at work was a complete blur. I rather sheepishly explained to my boss that I needed not only to finish work early that day but would also be missing for the next six days. I can only hold my hands up and say fair play to him as he was extremely understanding to say the least, given my late notification. He is a football man and fully understood the opportunity that had presented itself to me. He knew full well that when these chances in life present themselves, then you have got to grab hold of them and go for it.

Lunchtime arrived and I was off, back home to pack clobber for the trip along with toiletries, credit cards and cash. I just grabbed some of my clothes and stuffed them into the biggest holdall that I could find. I later realised to my horror that the one and only towel I had actually packed turned out to be one of the small hand towels that are exactly what they say on the tin; I had a towel for my hands for five days! What a start, and no wonder Donna insists on packing whenever we manage to get away somewhere.

I thought I had all bases covered so off I went back to work to say bye to my beloved and our colleagues. I would be lying if I said that I wasn't chuffed to bits with the fact that I was going on yet another great European adventure, but the feeling was also underlined with a big sense of guilt along with a huge pang of selfishness.

I strode back in to work with a subdued smile on my face. Donna was sat at the reception desk along with a couple of colleagues. As I approached the desk she looked up and delivered a huge bollocking and gave the impression that she wasn't too bothered who was around and could hear it either. Completely unprofessional and so out of character, not forgetting that this was a little embarrassing from my point of view.

The bollocking was aimed at me. In my haste to get ready I had only gone and picked up the wrong holdall, which had been given to her as a present by one of our daughters. It wasn't exactly a feminine sort of bag, it was just the biggest we had. I wasn't overly impressed by her rant, especially as it was delivered in front of our work-mates, but thankfully the slap around my legs didn't register with them too much. It's difficult to explain really but each and every time we know we are going to be apart, petty squabbles ensue.

In all the time we have been together we are lucky to say that we've had maybe three or four major arguments. For what it's worth, that is four too many as far as I'm concerned. It's impossible to believe but Donna and I almost never argue. Our kids will vouch for that. But I think the tensions of the upcoming trip and the thought of being apart had surfaced slightly that afternoon. She really was worried about the length of the journey that I was about to embark on.

Donna had done her very best to disguise it; after all she had coerced me into going, but looking back the poor girl must have been going through hell. My mixed emotions of the day could only have paled into insignificance in comparison to what she was feeling. Her mind must have been all over the place. What she was about to endure mentally throughout the next six days and nights, one can only imagine. I at least had other things and other people to help occupy my mind. I was going to be kept entertained on my latest great adventure with another European Cup Final destiny to look forward to. Donna only had the normal, run-of-the-mill things to keep her occupied while I was away.

2

Indigenous Reds

THIS IS just my account of one very special trip. A real trip that took approximately 152 hours and covered over 3,500 miles, by land and sea. Another reason to write this book was to try and give people a real insight as to how our indigenous supporters have a tremendous bond – a feeling of togetherness that comes from within and from being part of a group of people who have the same feelings towards each other, well mostly anyway. It's a feeling that is almost difficult to put into words. As the great man himself, Bill Shankly once said about Anfield's world-famous Kop and its inhabitants, 'There stand people with thousands of friends all about them, a sense of one big community, an extended family if you like.'

The masses who have stood together, laughed together and cried together in good times and bad are a unique, partisan and loyal band of brothers and sisters.

I had first entered this famous old terracing back in 1967 at the tender age of six years old. As was the norm when going to your first game, I went along with an older member of my family. My cousin Albert Fenn had been going to matches for many years and went on to become a member of the old 92 Club, for attending games at every stadium in all four divisions of the Football League. That took some doing, especially back in the 1960s and 70s when the transport infrastructure wasn't what it is today. I think the M6 was still cobbled! Not to mention the fact that football hooliganism was beginning to show its ugly face and was gaining momentum with each new season, so doing all of the grounds also took some balls.

Hooligans at the match may have been given a 1980s label but believe me, problems were around a little earlier than that. An old mate of mine often recalls tales of him being set upon and attacked by Leeds United fans on more than one occasion. It was during a weekend in London while visiting the capital for the 1974 Charity Shield game at Wembley. This tribal rivalry was beginning to surface a lot earlier than we were led to believe.

Albert had taken myself and my elder brother Paul to watch Liverpool play against the big and mighty Manchester United and their so-called legends of the day: the great George Best, the World Cup-winning Bobby Charlton, Denis Law and all. The family story ever since is that during the game, Paul had found the enormous crowd packed into the Kop too much and duly fainted. He was then swiftly crowd-surfed (this was happening long before music festivals) down to the perimeter of the pitch where the first-aiders of the St John Ambulance Brigade took care of him and quickly brought him to his senses. As I was his younger sibling it was deemed only right and proper that I should follow Paul to pitchside to where he was sitting so he could continue to look after me! We then proceeded to watch the Reds dispatch the Mancs 2-0 while sitting right by the corner flag, almost on the pitch itself.

The running joke is that Paul didn't like big crowds after that first match we had attended, so off he went to Goodison Park. I absolutely loved our day, was completely hooked and have been going back ever since. When I say that we watched the Reds play, I actually spent most of the afternoon watching the crowd instead of the game.

I sat there watching the swaying and singing human mass. I was in total awe as they exhibited so much support and passion for their beloved mighty Reds. This was a congregation that truly believed. A huge gathering that contained over 24,000 people all thought as one, sang as one and celebrated as one. As a child so young I had never witnessed anything like it before; I had never been so mesmerised in my short life. The noise, power and the strength that was generated down on to the pitch from the crowd was spine-tingling. All these people stood en masse on the Kop making this red and white army appear enormous and invincible. Even at that tender age I understood!

Right from that very first game, I was hooked. It was almost spell-binding watching the crowd. I was too young to really understand the football itself so I spent most of the match just focusing on the Kop. Right from the moment that we had first scuttled through the masses outside and eventually entered through the turnstiles behind The Albert, the pub on Walton Breck Road, I truly felt as if I understood the crowd. I felt I was one of them and wanted to be a part of this for ever more. I felt almost immediately that I belonged in this huge swaying, singing and supporting body of life.

Even after 50 years or more I still get the same old tingle walking up to the ground on matchdays.

Locals from all over the city and suburbs converge and congregate at the city's third cathedral. Some say that Anfield is the city's only, or at least first, cathedral, depending on how much religion has had an influence in your life and what it means to you. Before entering Anfield on a matchday most of the congregation would meet up with friends or family members in the local pubs around the ground or at the numerous watering holes that we have in the city centre.

Our stadium was converted, along with the rest of the top two divisions in English football, into an all-seated arena after the Lord Justice Taylor report's recommendations in 1990, following the Hillsborough disaster. His report also proposed the removal of metal fencing surrounding the pitch itself. Big ugly railings were designed to keep people from trying to run on to the pitch. In every stadium, fans were caged like animals.

It is without question that the stadiums we sit in today are for safer environments, but a direct result of this is that friends and family members are not always sat together watching the game anymore. The days of family gatherings inside the stadium are rare if not nigh-on impossible these days. When the Kop became seated in 1994, friends and families found themselves dispersed around the stand or even in other parts of Anfield in some cases. Therefore, their best chance to catch up and have a natter is in the local pubs before and after the match. It is in these places that you will bump into old faces, many of whom you may not have seen for a long time. A simple nod, a wink or a thumbs-up confirms that you are still a part of this huge family. It's an acknowledgement that seems to say, 'All right lad, nice to see you again!'

This is my attempt at trying to explain what that is all about. From a very young age, I was hearing stories from the early 1960s about when Bill Shankly first took the Reds abroad in 1964 to Iceland and then beyond. Europe was opening up for the Redmen.

I would often sit and listen in awe as older siblings of mates of mine would return home from their latest adventures with tales that would keep us enthralled for hours.

'Can't wait to grow up and be like them,' I would think to myself.

My very own first European adventure was away to CSKA Sofia of Bulgaria back in 1981, into eastern Europe and behind the old Iron Curtain at the age of 20. It was a very different place then to what it is now and was not the most welcoming of places.

The sight that shook me the most on this trip, and one that will stay with me forever, was the local community forming queues to shop. Long lines of people queuing for hours on end to buy something as basic as bread; the country appeared to be on its arse and had a population of very downbeat citizens who seemed resigned to their fate and simply got on with life. There appeared to be a very dark and gloomy cloud hanging over this city, even though if I remember correctly the weather was quite pleasant on this early March trip. I swear an old, burnt-out tank from the Second World War would not have looked out of place on a street corner here. I couldn't help but feel a little sense of guilt. There we were spending our cash on extravagances such as following the Reds around Europe and yet here were good people with not even a loaf on the table to feed their families.

Has socialism ever existed? I think not. I still see plenty of evidence to suggest that it hasn't on a daily basis, even today in work with so-called trade unionists and socialists as colleagues. Actually, in my experience in the workplace for over 40 years, these people are usually found to be the ones who look after themselves first. 'I'm all right Jack' underneath while portraying very different colours on the outside. Nice word though, socialism!

During our short stay in the Bulgarian capital, we were kept more or less under hotel arrest for most of the time that we spent there, although we did manage on more than one occasion to slip past our minders and venture out to take in the sights along with enjoying the local hospitality on offer. The house arrest was put in place so that the Sofian plod could keep an eye on us, not so much for our own safety but more likely that the local authorities were a little nervous as to the fact that a few hundred Scousers were on their manor. This, as I was reliably informed by one of the old faces who was travelling with us on that trip, was quite often the norm when roaming across Europe following the Reds. He had been on lots of excursions since the early days so when he spoke, you listened. It's called respect.

Our first night in Sofia was a long and hard one. The most likely and obvious cause of this was because of the copious amounts of dirt-cheap alcohol on offer in the hotel bar. Being a young buck of 20 years old on home leave from the navy with pockets full of cash, I was in my element and life at that time just couldn't have been any better for me.

Another unusual sight that has stayed with me from this trip was from inside the stadium on the night of the game. It was a little bizarre to say the least. There were around 500 Liverpool fans, and most were very much Scousers back in those days (none of the tourists that you see attending today), sandwiched between 60,000 CSKA supporters. The surreal image was that many thousands of the home fans were clad in army uniforms. That's what CSKA Sofia were back then – the Bulgarian national army team. That was one away ground where you hoped that no one would kick off and cause trouble. We wouldn't have stood a chance.

Today, I still see some of the same old faces who were present back then when I lost my Euro virginity. As the saying goes, 'you never forget your first time', which underlines my point perfectly. These locals have been travelling forever, not as a tourist doing their one and only – someone from a faraway land who wants to go to the game so they can tick it off their bucket list. No disrespect is intended to these people, as I know and understand the want and the need to see the Redmen in the flesh. It is indeed an ambition for them and millions of like-minded people around the world. If they can realise it then good luck to them, but I can guarantee it will come at a cost. It will be at the cost of a local. These people want to taste what the indigenous Redmen have been experiencing for many a year.

Apologies to these people but if they are ever fortunate enough to get a European away game under their belt then I can honestly say that they will only ever feel it as an outsider. That is in no way being racist, insular or even disrespectful, it's just a fact. They may well come in and have a look, enjoy it, even have the time of their life. No doubt they will go away with some amazing memories, photographs and stories to tell, with their bucket list ticked. But for the locals who travel, this is something that means a hell of a lot more than that. We feel it is our duty to be there, a calling if you like. There is a togetherness that can only ever be felt from within.

Although it may be difficult to understand for an outsider, it really is like being part of a very big family who look out for each other, watching each other's backs when things get tough.

You may not see each other for months on end, years even, but when paths do cross a simple nod or a wink is all it takes to bring you back into the bosom of the family.

Bill Shankly truly understood this unique bond and his work was for 'the people'. His words, not mine. This is a feeling and bond that no outsider or tourist will ever experience in its full entirety. To be fair, there are examples where the odd tourist has become a regular and fitted quite nicely into the fold but most are, and always will be, very much a visitor. I'm sure that other big clubs' local fans will have very similar relationships and feelings towards their own tourist supporters.

Some teams attract a lot more international visitors than others, I might add. Ourselves and the red Mancs have been the obvious main attractions for the overseas invasion for years, although other Premier League teams appear to be attracting some of their own tourist fans these days.

It is with great sadness and a very heavy heart that I must say that the sight of the local family gathering is decreasing with each passing season. Tickets for games appear to be getting in to the hands of the highest bidder these days. Because of this, the obvious result is fewer locals and more tourists. Football club owners not only view this as music to their ears, they must be hearing a complete philharmonic orchestra at its finest. Don't get me wrong, our owners have made serious investments in our club, but we must remember that's exactly what it is, an investment. Invest a little to make a lot, invest a lot to make more! They have made the right noises in a lot of places though, in the fact that they have frozen season ticket prices for a couple of seasons and they hand out free tickets to local schools. There are even some tickets available at heavily discounted rates to people with a Liverpool postcode but these are very few and far between.

People have remarked to me in recent years that on occasions the atmosphere isn't what it used to be at Anfield. The simple answer I always deliver is that it was the locals who created the atmosphere. Sadly, these good local people are very much in decline, almost a breed in danger of extinction. When I refer to locals, I am talking about the very people for whom our club was formed, the inhabitants of the city that our club represents and resides in. The majority of people from Liverpool cannot get to see the team that represents them, not without paying through the nose anyway.

I recently had an uncomfortable experience at Anfield when I had a Norwegian lady crying on my shoulder. There were real tears in her eyes as she began telling me how disappointed she was that she had travelled so many miles and spent so much money in order to sample the atmosphere that is created inside Anfield, by the world-famous Kop. She was so upset that on this occasion the atmosphere was rather flat. This lady had been sat there with her phone out trying to film the Kop in all its glory. By the way, all the time she had her device out filming the crowd, the game was in full flow so she wasn't even watching what was happening on the pitch. I offered no apologies whatsoever when I said to her, 'Atmosphere is created, not videoed.'

A few years ago, I was fortunate enough to go on a transatlantic journey across the pond to watch New York Yankees play baseball. Although it was not the sole purpose of my visit to the States, an opportunity had presented itself to visit the world-famous Yankee Stadium. This just had to be on the to-do list when visiting the Big Apple. It sounds hypocritical, I know, but the stadium itself was no more than 30 per cent full on the day that Donna and I decided to call in. I would never have dreamt of trying to gain admission if it was a full house or a game of some importance that a local should be attending.

Apart from how boring and stop-start that afternoon's entertainment was, there was one thing that stood out that day. I am still trying to decide whether I was alarmed, saddened or amused by what I witnessed during the game.

At one end of the stadium was a huge HD scoreboard. It was 103ft^2 to be exact. In between the countless adverts that kept running during the game, or certainly appeared to do so, every now and then a huge pair of Mickey Mouse hands would appear on the screen encouraging the crowd to clap hands and generate some support and atmosphere for their team. Create some atmosphere! Believe me when I say, 'All things American are coming to our game.' Also believe me when I say that I sincerely hope that I am long gone before we ever need things like Mickey Mouse to help generate and create some noise and atmosphere at the Anfield cathedral. Long gone!

3

The Money Men

OUR BEAUTIFUL game and from a more personal point of view our beautiful team have been taken away from the local supporters; kidnapped, hijacked, call it what you want, but they've been taken away and given to the world. The locals are being squeezed out with every passing season. Although not alone in its practices, a certain TV company has been a major player in that since the Premier League's launch back in 1992, very successfully it must be said. The money men were involved right from the very start of the Premier League era but the bubble cannot keep getting bigger and bigger; surely it has got to burst at some point.

Once upon a time a certain Scotsman from just up the East Lancs Road said, 'Once you shake hands with the devil you pay the price. TV is God at the moment!'

The bubble has got a whole lot bigger since Fergie voiced those words of warning back in 2011.

To put it another way, we have sold our soul along with every other Premier League team to the highest bidder. We are not alone in this but Liverpool Football Club were and indeed still are, a major player in taking this product global. For a long time now, Liverpool, along with many other of the big teams, have been enjoying their pre-season preparations on very distant shores, whipping up support and selling our badge in every corner of the globe. We are all guilty of chasing the dollars with not so much as a thought to those left in their wake. Clubs may well be getting bigger, better and richer but the direction football is going in certainly doesn't sting any less. In fact it hurts a little more each season with constant fixture changes to Friday nights, Monday nights, Saturday nights and even sometimes Sunday mornings. The travelling local fans are at the very bottom of the food chain when it comes to consideration.

These money men have come in and commandeered our beloved working-class pastime. They are huge in the world of business and are simply out to make dollars. They may make the right noises and pay a certain amount of lip service to the naive who listen. No one could ever argue that our custodians haven't put their money where their mouth is and supported the club. They've developed the stadium and surrounding area and anybody who knows or lives in the Anfield area of Liverpool will have seen a huge change for the better in recent years, although this is still a work in progress.

The expansion of the stadium itself is extremely impressive and was so desperately needed. The academy training complex expansion in Kirkby is in full swing and once completed it will house the first team squad, alongside the under-23s and the junior squads within a world-class training facility. How inspirational will that be for the young players coming through the ranks?

The owners have also invested heavily on top players, no question about that. Yet locally, there is still a feeling of some resentment towards these people. They haven't so much given the locals a team to be proud of, certainly not in the Bill Shankly mould. It's more a case of giving our 500 million supporters worldwide a team to be proud of. I completely understand, that's how it is today, and maybe we're a victim of our own success.

Without doubt the game has moved on to another level since the start of the Premier League, and the product we see these days and the whole circus that accompanies it is incomparable to the football from bygone eras, but at what cost?

I know that this money game we have now has gone too far and it can never be reversed, which means the good old days will never be back. Football is now a huge cake and for sure these investors demand the biggest slice. What bewilders me is just how big a cake they want to bake, and just how much anyone can eat. The power-brokers want to create the biggest and strive to get it, driven by dollar signs. Which continent these investors come from is completely irrelevant. Each and every one of them is ultimately here for the money. They may well bang on about knowing the club they have purchased, and being aware of its great history, values and traditions; they may say how much they love the club and have been a true supporter all their lives, but it's pure lip service.

Anyone who thinks differently has an awful lot to learn. They need to wake up and smell the roses, or should that be 'smell the scent of the vanishing local'? The local supporter who used to go to the game with his dad or with his kids, and who helped in so many ways to build our club into what it is today, is being increasingly marginalised.

The players themselves are equally as guilty. The bigger the cake they see being baked gives them the right to say, 'Well, we supply the main ingredients for the cake so therefore we deserve a larger slice of it.' A fair shout, I suppose, but just how much of the big cake these people demand is baffling.

I know full well that footballers give up a lot of time to help endorse charities and do more than their fair share when it comes to personal appearances, but exactly how many big houses, cars, yachts and all the fancy trimmings does somebody need to own in order to live an extremely good life?

How many lifetimes would they each need to live to be able to spend what they amass? Each and every one of us is under a certain amount of pressure to ensure that we are in a position to be able to leave our offspring something for when we have gone, but these people earn enough to keep their future generations for eternity and beyond. Their kids will never have to lift a finger to survive. I am not singling out footballers' children here, and I suppose anyone born into wealth or with a silver spoon in their mouth would have great difficulty with reality. But then they won't need to live in the real world so why should they worry?

My point is that if all of the cake eaters would just lower their demands, even by only a small percentage, and maybe go on a sort of cash diet, then surely that would be of benefit to far more people. Maybe that money could be filtered back down to fans in the shape of improvements such as cheaper tickets.

As it stands, the money men involved need to bake the biggest cake in order to attract the best players and pay the biggest salaries. This increases their chances of a bigger return on their investment if things go to plan and their businesses are successful. Serious money men don't often make mistakes when investing and they are acutely aware that the bigger the investment they make then the bigger the chances of good returns are. Don't forget the fact that they also need to keep a little of the premiums aside for themselves and their shareholders.

It is a vicious circle that has been created within football, which was once the domain of the working classes and a release valve at the end of every week. It was somewhere to go and shout and scream as much as you like, along with thousands of other like-minded people. I sometimes stop to think how the average Joe Bloggs releases his steam these days.

Who picks up the bill for all this? Maybe the locals who can't get in to their home stadiums anymore so therefore need to subscribe to the monster TV channels in order to watch their team play. Their hometown team, who earn their living and ply their trade just around the corner from where they live.

Proof of this is very much in evidence on matchday itself. Small groups of young kids can be found milling around the stadium listening to the atmosphere bursting out from inside, standing there, listening, dreaming of one day maybe even getting in themselves. So very sad.

Mr Shankly, I'm convinced, will be turning cartwheels, never mind spinning in his grave. Most, if not all of my generation and indeed our forefathers, were the most important thing to Shankly. The masses who stood and supported the Reds through the storm, through the wind and rain, good times and bad, week in, week out. We were as important to

Shankly as the team itself. He wanted nothing more in life but to 'make the people happy'. That phrase is etched upon his very deserving statue situated outside the Kop on Walton Breck Road.

By the way, several decades after the great man made that comment it was then unashamedly stolen, taken across Stanley Park and used by David Moyes. Well, we all know how that ended.

The so-called day-trippers or the tourist supporters attend games in their thousands these days. They are the big spenders in town and because of this the locals can't get a look in. My big pet hate now at matches is the half-and-half scarf with both teams emblazoned on it along with the date of the game, bought as a souvenir.

You can spot a local a mile off. They won't be wearing many colours, if any at all. The locals who helped enormously to build the club's reputation are simply not wanted any more, because they don't spend in the club shops or in the stadium's hospitality lounges.

I must add that Liverpool are not alone in this working model; many top-flight clubs are in the same position and are all competing for a share of the global market.

All this aside, as much as it pains me to see the way football has evolved, you can only give huge credit to FSG for having the investment, commitment and foresight. Without this we would have been left far behind the other top clubs.

Rant over – for now!

4

Technophobe

THIS TRIP was unusual in the fact that this was the first one that I was going to be travelling on alone, in the sense that previously I have always travelled with friends or family, and sometimes both. More often than not I have travelled with Donna, who is my wife, best friend and soul mate. This was going to be my first trip with people I had never met before. But, as the saying goes, 'There's no such thing as strangers, only friends you haven't met.'

I am not the best when it comes to technology. I can give you a hand with building a house, basic plumbing, or even basic electrics, but show me a computer and I'm not that educated or even that interested. Don't get me wrong, I can surf and delete history with the best of them, but I imagine all fellas can do that! I remember my elder brother Paul teaching me how to do it many years ago.

By nature, I am a nosey kind of bloke; not into other people's business mind, more that I don't want to miss anything. I like to stay awake when travelling whether it be on a bus, in a car, on a boat, train or even on planes. I am afraid of missing a minute. Admittedly there's not much to see when you're 30,000 feet up in a plane other than people-watching. We all do it!

I have often wished I could sleep like the rest of the boys and girls on these trips. Some of the positions they managed to fall asleep in would cripple me for life. Another reason I am awake more than most is that unfortunately for me I inherited my dad's sleep gene. He's not keen on his kip and was often heard wandering around the house at some unearthly hour of the morning.

My ignorance about everything techno was annoyingly proven in my attempt at writing down my memoirs from this latest adventure.

During the times when the taxi was quiet and with not much to see apart from fields and cows, I decided to put pen to paper, or should I say letters on to a Word document. More basically and to the point, letters on to a phone. Motorway driving to me is possibly the most tedious way of travelling and I've done it on and off professionally for 35 years or more. Since the vast majority of our trip was spent on motorways crossing different countries, it was an ideal opportunity to try to achieve an ambition.

I thought I would start by writing down a few details of events that had gone before us and also to prepare for anything else that may unfold ahead, to break the boredom when the rest of the little angels travelling with me were sound asleep. Being a technophobe, getting these words on to my phone in itself was a major challenge. I thought I was getting the hang of things and therefore tried to be smart by creating a second diary, so if anything went wrong I would have something to fall back on. A little insurance just in case anything I had written disappeared off into cyberspace, wherever that is. I will add this though, if the Reds were ever to play in cyberspace, I can guarantee you will find a band of merry men and women there to support them!

I'm honest enough and sorry to say that all of Donna's tutoring on anything techno over the years was totally wasted. My first attempt to log things had taken around seven hours to write and done exactly what I had feared. Vanished, gone without a trace. Off into the big dark hole never to be seen again.

The time in between pit stops, drinking, eating and much merriment was ideal for rewriting what I had lost. I must have completed at least another six hours' writing by the time I put my phone down as we entered yet another service station. Fed, watered and back on board the taxi, I had more material from this stop to note down. Guess what? The whole lot had disappeared once more! After a tirade of unprintable language from me I regained my composure and it wasn't a problem, I thought, as I've always got the backup journal.

But only an idiot makes the same mistake twice and expects different results. Surprise surprise, that didn't work either. The second backup had disappeared too!

I'm sure Donna had mentioned something about saving stuff at previous home tutorials. Whoops.

5

The Travelling Companions

IT WAS a beautiful early summer's day in the parish of Anfield. The date was 23 May 2018; the time was 6pm. Various mixes of Liverpool supporters were arriving for the mammoth road trip that would lead this merry, hopeful and oh so happy band of brothers and sisters off on another European adventure towards Kyiv in the east of Ukraine.

The congregation was a mix of dads and lads, I think two couples, teams of boys, family members and a couple of solo travellers, of which I was one. Outside the world-famous watering hole known as The Arkles on the junction of Anfield Road and Arkles Lane, four eight-seater taxis had arrived to pick up this merry band of fans and whisk us all down the road to Kyiv. There was to be no walking about stretching our legs or going to the toilet on these bad boys.

By down the road I mean 1,729 miles, straight run 30 hours or so. But this was never going to be a straight or easy run.

Four taxis meant eight drivers in total, all good lads, and can you believe that seven of them were Evertonians! Jokes were plentiful and fired machine-gun-like in the direction of these fellas for much of the trip and very much in the vein of, 'Only chance of getting into Europe, boys?' Or, 'Are you coming with us to see what it's like travelling abroad with your team, boys?' Then there was, 'You're coming with us coz you don't ever watch the blue shite abroad.'

There was banter aplenty but fair play to these lads, they took it all on the chin and tried to give a little back. They had a huge job ahead of them and each in their own way got through with huge credit.

The drivers of our little taxi were two lads called Paul and Terry. Paul Vernon was a Blue and quickly became known as 'Three Amp'. His composure would fly out of the window very easily and very quickly. I could never picture him as a police negotiator or in any other role that required a little diplomacy.

Three Amp was 28 years old and a decent fella who seemed to have a lot going for him with a young fiancée on his arm and two boys of pre-school age. He was from the Netherton area of Liverpool and like me, upon leaving school, went off to see the world by joining the services. His choice was the RAF and he was stationed down in Buckinghamshire for a few years during his service. While there, Three Amp achieved the enviable accolade of being the top recruit in physical training. A big lad who you wouldn't bet against. These days he earns his crust as an overhead line engineer for one of the railway companies.

Three Amp told us that the very first game he attended was Everton v Middlesbrough back in 1999, which finished in a 2-0 away win for Boro. He mentioned that he found a pound coin on the way out of Goodison Park, which must have been the highlight of his day. Some things never change! I must say that I have never come across anyone like Three Amp who gets wound up so quickly and sees problems around every corner, or should I say imagines them? He was so wound up at times that I thought he was about to explode on more than one occasion. Talk about a coiled spring.

Maybe I'm wrong, but my school of thought is that I try not to worry about things too much until they happen. What's the point? On the other hand, the mentality of Three Amp was to think about them, how to avoid them, have a contingency plan and stay one step ahead. He got himself so wound up over the slightest thing.

His co-pilot was a bloke named Terry Casey, a 34-year-old from Birkenhead with a wife and three kids; he was the one Liverpool-supporting driver, quite surprisingly. This was despite the fact that Terry's family were all Blue. I mentioned earlier in this book that the team you normally end up supporting is the first one you go and watch live. This normally comes from the family member or a friend who first took you to a game, from your mates in the street or from your peers in the school playground.

You never forget your first team and you stick with them, good times and bad, no matter what. A divorce is never an option. Some people have been known to swap but these occurrences are extremely rare. Both of Terry's parents, along with his other family members, were Everton fans. Terry did mention that he was initiated into Goodison Park back when he was a young boy but simply hated it. He couldn't explain why, but he hated the place. After a chance visit to Anfield he was immediately smitten. Love at first sight you might say; some things are just meant to be. I also sensed that there may have been an element of rebel in the young Terry. My youngest son is also a Blue, I expect for the very same reasons.

After leaving school, Terry sought a career in the army, the King's Regiment to be exact, also known as the Scouse battalion. Another decent lad, he also possessed a talent for mimicking accents.

Both drivers were ex-servicemen, both were organised, both were worldly wise and both were as hard as f**k to boot. We were going to be in safe hands, I just knew it. Both were also extremely good company to say the least.

Our drivers gave me the impression that the boys and girls who protect our homeland really are a methodical bunch. It's a result of all that military training, I assume, although I strongly suspect that these people need to be cut from a certain cloth. No doubt different levels of being methodical and organised exist within that group so on that note I'd say that on a scale of one to ten, Three Amp was definitely a ten; everything had to be planned. No off-the-cuff, spontaneous actions in his life. I often chuckled to myself that I bet even his meal times, bath times, shopping trips, family outings, and even sex, had to be delivered on time and with precision.

Terry was also organised but didn't show any of the anxieties that Three Amp displayed and, more worryingly, harboured. He appeared to take everything as it came, although without doubt a certain amount of planning and forward-thinking was high on his agenda. I also got the impression that Terry could be a handful if necessary – the sort of fella I would back in most one-on-one scuffles.

It eventually came to light that initially, Terry was really nervous about driving abroad and tried to disguise his concerns. He did a reasonably good job in doing that, so much so that I think I was the only one to get on to him. I got a little sense of uncertainty along the way once we had crossed the Channel and began driving on the wrong side of the road but I kept my observations to myself.

Terry 'fessed up the day after our return about his driving reservations. It was a different story coming home; he was throwing the taxi around as if he was Lewis Hamilton tearing up and down Silverstone on a practice day. But he did a really great job.

This boy had seen some shit in his life; apart from coming from a Blue family he was also an ex-soldier who had been on the front line during the troubles in Helmand Province in Afghanistan. Some of the stories he told us traumatised me, so I hate to think what it must do to the boys and girls involved in all of that madness. One little tale he mentioned was that one day he and his colleagues were out on patrol and had come under attack from the Taliban. Terry and his comrades had spotted some of the protagonists running into a shed or garage. Their orders from above were to return fire and they then basically proceeded to flatten the building in question.

After the battle had ceased and the gunfire had fallen silent, they were ordered to investigate the building and its remains. I will leave it to your imagination but the Taliban were not the only occupants of said building on that unfathomable day. We've all seen stuff in the movies but try and comprehend what that is like in real life. Babies, children, young and old;

sadly it's classed as collateral damage. I seriously doubt I could ever get over something like that.

Terry wouldn't readily volunteer this information but would chat when asked. I think it was starting to play on a few of the lads' minds, so questions of this nature became less frequent and thankfully the topic faded away. Some of his tales really would interfere with my sleep, or at least contribute to the lack of it in the coming days.

If ever you find yourself going on a monster trip for whatever reason, take my advice – grab yourself an ex-squaddie, airman, sailor, whatever. These fellas are priceless. You need a shite; they've got the toilet roll. Sweaty bollocks; they have the wet wipes. Hungry; they've got food stashed in all compartments.

They are mentally super-tough too. Watching the rest of the convoy achieving varying degrees of merriment while staying completely dry and sober for six days or so can't have been easy. Maybe it's a task used in the SAS recruitment process, but if not then trust me it should be. These fine chaps had willpower in abundance and were prepared for anything.

They were so well organised it makes me wonder how the rest of us had managed this far. Plus, if it ever goes off in your vicinity then these men were the sort you would want, or need in your corner.

My respect for these people who serve and protect increased on a daily basis while in their company.

Also on board were two brothers, Paul and Karl Carney. These boys hailed from Anfield and were both professional kids. Young, good looking, sharply dressed, honest and decent boys who were a credit to their parents. They were lads you could never envisage having any problems with at all if your daughter were to bring either of them home.

Paul was 33 years old and was an active serviceman. He was married and living in Lincolnshire with his young family of one little child and another one on the way. Paul's work in the RAF took him to that part of the world, although he would still travel home to watch the Reds play whenever he could.

Karl was the younger brother by three years, living with his partner and no kids on the horizon. I couldn't blame him as his job took him around the world on a regular basis. Karl told me that his first visit to Anfield was back in 1993. He had gone along to the game with his dad and grandad, just how it used to be.

Coincidentally, the first game Karl went to was also against Manchester United, the same as me but many years later. His first visit to Anfield was during the season that was to be the Kop's last year as a standing terrace. His dad had lifted him up on to one of the metal crush barriers so he could get a better view of the match. He told me that all he can remember is hearing the crowd chant 'Who the f**k are Man United' and decided to join in, only to receive a crack around the head off his dad. Karl was only around seven years old at the time. He and Paul appeared to have something nice going on between them, which was great to see.

I can honestly say we got the long straw as far as the seating was allocated for each taxi as the only other fella on board our little motor was a bloke named Jamie. He was in his early 40s with the attitude of someone half his age. Initially I thought it was probably best to leave Jamie's surname anonymous in this book, simply because I didn't think he would want his name echoed around as some sort of wrong 'un. After having a recent chat with him, his shrug of the shoulders attitude told to me that he wasn't bothered who knew. Jamie May was undoubtedly the star of the show, the main character and without question at the epicentre of most things.

Jamie is a big family man who has seven kids, all with his childhood sweetheart. They are still together, so I'd call that a result. You will learn a lot more about Jamie as this story unfolds.

I have mentioned on more than one occasion that I have been blessed in life to have been on countless excursions around England and Europe following our beloved Reds. In varying careers as a sailor, factory worker, publican, guest house proprietor and HGV driver, I used to think that I've met every kind of character that was ever made. I have met Jamie's kind before but these boys are very thin on the ground. Lots of fellas like to think there is an element of rogue in them, and many have experienced things that would qualify them to claim so, but Jamie is Premier League and Champions League qualification every year, no question. I'm not saying his sort are on top, just serious contenders. If not on top themselves, then they have ample supplies of contacts from people who are. Serious players indeed.

Jamie told me that he was from Belmont Road in Anfield. He loved growing up in that part of town because the place was predominantly Red. When still at junior school his family had decided to relocate to Walton, the largely Blue side of town. Jamie was lost, so used to seeing Reds all around him and yet there he was surrounded by Blues. He said it was like living in a foreign country.

Fortunately, it wasn't too long before Jamie stumbled upon a couple of other immigrant families who were Reds too. He and his new-found friends would venture out across Stanley Park on matchdays, where they were to go on and perfect the art of bunking in to the ground. They would duck under the turnstiles, leap over them and double click (when two people gain access through one click of the turnstile). Occasionally they would even get in through unlocked doors. In fact they used every way they could think of in order to gain access into the church as Jamie called Anfield. He was simply doing as his ma had told him and went to church every week like a good boy with his mates. By the time he had reached the mature age of eight years old he was a master of the trade, a fully qualified bunker! He would never miss a game after his first visit to this place of worship.

Jamie's first match was when he was five years old as the Reds faced Arsenal in 1983. Like so many before him, he had gone to Anfield with his dad and uncle.

Liverpool beat Arsenal 3-1 that day with goals from Ian Rush, Graeme Souness and the King himself, Kenny Dalglish. How could you not fall in love with that?

Jamie is so far off the radar he is simply immeasurable. He is a bloke who is devoted to his clan, has high morals and his values are in all the right places. He would kill and die for his family in a heartbeat, is protective of those around him and always looks out for friends, old and new. He also hates litter bugs.

He features quite predominantly in this book, simply because he seemed to be at the centre of most things. The main protagonist, you could say. Jamie is the first to buy a round at the bar, the first to slip a couple of pennies into the hand of a homeless person, the first to dish out a bollocking if someone discards their litter and the first to cover your arse if things are going pear-shaped.

Maybe it's his alter ego from his normal and respectable day job, but he is an absolute nut. Not in a crazy, aggressive, couldn't give a f**k sort of way; more with a cool, calm and collected attitude, weighing things up constantly. Well, that's when he is actually awake. Jamie likes his sleep.

Nothing is off the table with this boy; nothing is impossible, no fence too high, so he'll try. Jamie is afraid of nothing and you just can't help but love him.

Personally, within the six days I'd spent in his very close company I felt I'd known him all my life, and what's more I trusted him. I'm certain my other travelling companions felt exactly the same way about him too. A 21st-century Artful Dodger, if you like.

6

The Artful Dodgers

I MENTIONED earlier that I had met Jamie's kind before. One scally does spring to mind – probably the person most like Jamie that I've ever met – from a trip to watch the European Cup semi-final back in 1981, away to Bayern Munich. That trip was also by road but was on a luxury coach; well, a coach that you could walk around on anyway. I had gone with an old mate of mine, Craig Davenport.

We had both unexpectedly found ourselves at home on leave at the same time. This was a rarity in itself as Craig was also in the Merchant Navy so therefore our paths rarely crossed when off duty, although that season we did somehow manage to get three European away trips under our belt together: CSKA Sofia, Bayern Munich and then Paris for the final against Real Madrid. As the history books will tell you, that wasn't too bad a season at all.

Heading out to Munich, we found ourselves on a coach full of proper head cases. We departed from the Wavertree clock in the very early hours of the Monday morning for the game in Germany on the Wednesday night. One of our travelling companions on that trip was a young buck who went by the name of Babs.

Babs was so named because he was the youngest child of a big family from the tough district of Kirkby, which is about six miles north on the outskirts of Liverpool. This town was built for the city population's overspill in the 1950s and 60s and some have even called it 'the bastard cousin' of Liverpool.

Not a place for the faint-hearted, it is sometimes said. This sprawling estate has spawned many good people and famous faces over the years from both sport and the arts, including a pair of European Cup-winning captains – Phil Thompson, a Reds legend, and Dennis Mortimer of Aston Villa. They attended the same Kirkby school – Brookfield High. How many towns can boast that, let alone council estates or more uniquely schools? Two local boys from the same patch lifting 'Old Big Ears', both as captains as well.

Babs knew all the tricks and plenty more that others didn't. On one particular stop-over heading south towards Munich we arrived for the night in the city of Heidelberg. There were about a dozen or so of the boys out and about enjoying the German hospitality. It was all very pleasant; we were sat in a bar having a nice quiet drink and getting along in great measures with our hosts. We had been enjoying the local scene for over an hour when Babs suddenly announced that he was going back to our hotel. No explanation was given as to why, he just upped and left. Nothing was said and we just carried on socialising as we were before.

He had been gone for no more than two or three minutes when all hell let lose within this establishment. There was lots of pointing and shouting, mainly in our direction, which was rather worrying to say the least.

The German waiters all seemed to be carrying little money pouches around their waists, a sort of bumbag that certain people wear these days. It transpired later that Babs had pickpocketed one of these waiters and absconded with his wallet. Amid all the shouting and commotion that followed, the electric security shutters were quickly lowered. There we were, inside an impromptu lock-in, all within what seemed like no more than a few minutes. We sat there in total confusion.

The German plod were swiftly on the scene and they soon proceeded to empty the bar one by one, then they set up an identification parade in the little street outside the bar. The line-up consisted of Scousers only. Silence descended over our little posse as the realisation dawned upon us just how serious this was. None of us could even guess as to what the problem was. The fact that the German authorities were out in numbers and had us Scousers in their sights quickly brought us to our senses. The waiter slowly and painfully scoured the line-up and as he came up close to me, shouted, 'Ja, ja.' He nodded towards the armed police and that was it – I was spun around, shoved aggressively against the wall, arms and legs spread wide apart and unceremoniously searched. I can't say I was surprised to find myself sobering up very quickly indeed, especially as one of the officers held his gun to the back of my head while his colleague searched me.

You cannot begin to imagine the thoughts that race through your mind when someone has you in that position.

Would he have used the gun? Looking back, I very much doubt it, but it doesn't stop your arse falling apart at the time. Being young and naive, I truly didn't know what to expect. He probably wouldn't have shot me but I'm sure he was ever so capable and more than willing to give me a crack around my head with his gun if I had offered any resistance to his advances. It goes without saying that nothing was found on my person to link me to the crime, but that didn't stop the police dishing out a lesson, or should I say a message.

I swear, not one of us knew anything about what was going on. Eventually and thankfully, the waiter changed his mind about pinning it on me and we were all sent on our way with a flea in our ear, and shite running down my legs to be honest. The boys left the scene of the crime rather sharply and it was straight off back to the hotel to keep our heads down and avoid any more dramas, plus I could clean myself up too.

The local authorities were quickly brought up to speed that there may be one or two naughty Scousers in town. The plod appeared to be multiplying by the minute all through the city centre streets as we walked towards our abode for the night. The boys were understandably pretty wound up at having their night cut short, not to mention the fact that we were being treated as villains. During our walk back up through the city's main street we were approached by a couple of local Germans intent on giving us some verbals. These young bucks had picked the wrong moment to create any tension and were both swiftly dispatched into a beautiful statue-laden fountain along our route. With the least amount of force, I must add. It was a tension defuser actually as the sight of these two German scallies emerging from beneath the water fully clothed and dripping wet through was quite funny.

About 15 minutes or so later we were entering the sanctuary of our hotel for the night and the sight that greeted us was one that gave me mixed emotions to put it ever so mildly. I didn't know whether to laugh or start throwing punches around. Sat there in the hotel lobby was Babs, sitting there so relaxed with a big grin on his face. Beside him were at least ten full crates of lager, and they were just for starters. 'Where the f**k have you lot been?' he shouted over.

'Getting abused by some Gestapo bastards,' I shouted back. 'Why didn't you tell us what you were up to?' one of the lads asked him. 'Because the less you knew the less you could tell,' was his response, as he handed out the beers. Not that we weren't trusted to keep quiet, more of a covering all angles on his behalf; loose lips sink ships as the saying goes.

That was another party that went on long into the night. One of the lads with us on that trip got to host his own little private party that night with an army of prostitutes. I guess he felt his cash could be put to another use because of the amount he had saved on free beer, with Babs playing barman for the rest of the night.

Having met both Babs and Jamie and having spent a fair amount of time in their close company, it was only natural I suppose to presume that both boys had graduated from the same school of artful dodgery, both with Masters, possibly even with honours.

Babs was up to anything and everything, and after looting various jewellery shops and sports clothing establishments across Germany he was eventually arrested and consequently deported after trying to enter Munich's old Olympic Stadium with a forged ticket. Poetic justice, you may say.

Well let me tell you this – these boys think outside the box. Babs had stashed his wares away into a bank safety deposit box that he had purchased back in Heidelberg, well before his impending arrest. Unfortunately we never got to see Babs again on this trip after he had got himself nicked. A few days after returning home, I made contact with one of his brothers to enquire as to Babs's wellbeing. Apparently he had still not returned home and was working his way around Europe on his own until the heat had cooled down in Germany. He was grafting away in and around Scandinavia until things had quietened down. Babs was then planning on slipping back into Germany undetected, then heading back to Heidelberg and clearing out his safety deposit box. His loot was safe in there and as long as he remained undetected by the border authorities then he would be okay.

They had no knowledge of his safety deposit box, but because he had recently been deported for the forged ticket offence he had to keep on his toes and stay clever.

I later learned that Babs's plan had been executed to perfection. He had even managed to earn a little more, bouncing around Scandinavia before eventually making it across the border and back into Germany to retrieve his loot.

7

Scouse Connections

THE OWNER of the taxi company who organised this trip was another fella named Terry. This Terry, unlike our driver, was a proper Blue. The tattoo on his arm of Prince Rupert's Tower, which is Everton's badge, looked suspiciously new. I would swear that he'd had it done especially for the trip. Blue Terry was driving bus number two with Kev as his second driver. Kev seemed a decent lad from the few conversations I had with him, although he also was a Blue.

Unfortunately, due to the deteriorating relationship between the younger Reds and Blues, these days there is a new-found attitude towards each other. A wall appears to have been erected and indeed gets a little higher with each new season. The ripple effect is that both Everton and Liverpool have supporters of all living generations that are turning their backs on each other. Quite uniquely, the city still boasts the fact that we have mixed families of both persuasions but when it comes to strangers, then it is quite obvious that the love just isn't there anymore. I have found myself on many occasions giving the Blue boys a wide berth, even when holidaying abroad with my family and friends.

Reds and Blues, once upon a time, were all over each other; if you met as strangers on holiday, at home or abroad, then more often than not you would end up being drinking partners for the rest of the trip, but not now. How sad is that?

I know for certain that I am not alone in this practice. To some people, Reds and Blues mixing really is a tinder box, so much so that even when I am in the company of my brothers or any other Blue members of the family we try to avoid all conversations about football. I guarantee it will get out of control, especially if there is booze involved, not in a physical way but sometimes words can do much more damage. It's best to stay away and leave the subject alone. We have plenty of other things to moan about anyway. I will say a little more about the Merseyside relationship at the end of this book.

Travelling in owner Terry's taxi were what appeared to be a nice gentle mix of dad and lads, a young couple (I so wish Donna could have made it) and fellas who were just reliving their youth. 'Growing old is compulsory, growing up is voluntary,' I've always said. Another one I like is, 'You don't stop because you die, you die because you stop.'

One of the dad and lad teams travelling in Terry's taxi were Dave and his young son George, who was maybe around 12 years old. Whenever the taxis stopped, most of the other passengers would make a little fuss of George. If the two had a quiet moment together you could see them laughing, chatting or even having a hug. They had a great relationship which was wonderful to see. These two were in a position that thousands of others would have given almost anything to be in. A dad and lad on a European away trip – it doesn't get any better than that. Most if not all of this taxi's inhabitants would have blended in anywhere really. People and things quickly get nicknames and this vehicle became known as the 'dad and lad' taxi.

Taxi number three was laden with travellers who according to Scousers seemed to be mainly wools (people not from the city). I am one of these, although I like to feel that I was adopted and accepted into the fold many decades ago. I was born in Chester but from day one I lived and was brought up in Ellesmere Port, a little town about ten miles or so from Liverpool. When I was 16 I decided to spread my wings and explore the world beyond our shores.

Upon leaving school I went off and joined the Merchant Navy based in Mann Island down on Liverpool's waterfront, adjacent to the Pier Head. It was there that I first started to immerse myself properly in the Scouse way. My cousin Albert had taken me to my first game back in 1967, so from such an early age I had considered myself Scouse, or a Scouse wannabe at least. Now I felt like one of them; I certainly didn't feel, act or resemble anything else really.

Being a seaman registered in Liverpool, I suppose it was inevitable that most of my voyages across the seven seas would be in the company of Scousers. Liverpool people have a long history in maritime matters; after all Liverpool was once the busiest shipping port in the UK. It was only natural that young boys and girls from the area would want to follow in their forefathers' footsteps and explore the world outside their city, beyond their horizon. It's in their DNA.

It was during my navy days that I contracted the wanderlust bug. My thirst for travel just grew and grew. Following the Redmen around the UK and beyond just fed my bug more and more. What a perfect way to kill two birds with one stone. From my middle to late teens onwards I was travelling the world for a living and travelling the world for fun; utopian days indeed. Was there any better way of feeding my lust?

This bug enveloped me so much that whenever I came home on leave from the navy the first thing I would do is find out where the Reds were playing and make plans to be there. Playing at home, away or even abroad wasn't an issue. There were times when I would arrive home on leave and within a couple of days or so I would be off again, watching the Reds wherever they may have been playing. I vividly remember my dad chewing my ear off on more than one occasion, 'You've only just come home son, why you going away again? Stay home and save some money soft lad, you'll need it one day.'

At that age all I needed was cash on the hip and somewhere to go and spend it. The one day that Pop kept making reference to was decades away as far as I was concerned. A whole lifetime away. How often have you heard the saying 'live for today'? That has been my line of thought and attitude from a very early age, and although it is a little tamed these days, I still try and keep it in mind.

Pop wasn't into the football, so he couldn't understand the need to go to games at every opportunity. He was more into the horses, not in a gambling way, although he would have a little flutter if he was in the British Legion with his mates on a Saturday afternoon. He liked the show jumping stuff that Harvey Smith and his chums used to get up to. I know his love of these animals came from his own childhood. My grandfather Peter was from Italian parentage and his mum and dad had migrated and settled in Chester in the early 1900s. When old enough, my grandad had started up an ice cream business in the city and in those days he would pull his cart full of goodies around the city by horse. He had three horses and naturally Pop had become quite attached to these powerful beasts in his early childhood.

Trust me, because of his lack of interest in the beautiful game, my brothers and I never tired of letting Pop know how much of a girl we thought he was (not a sexist comment at all; things were different back then as the game was dominated by males). I must add that this was done as far away as possible out of arm's reach. We may have been mischievous and a little cheeky at times, but we weren't stupid. Pop had a decent dig on him if he managed to land one on you.

I can vouch for this as I often copped what either of my brothers warranted as well as paying my own dues. I am the second-born of three boys and was quite often caught in the middle but to be truthful, I was probably the main protagonist most of the time. I'm not saying that Pop was abusive, I would never say that. We were probably quite deserving any time rough justice was dished out, after all we were three cheeky young bucks learning our way. It didn't do me or my brothers any harm at all and if anything it taught us good lessons.

I am eternally thankful that I never took Pop's advice back then, and stayed home and saved some cash. I would have missed out on so much; all of those wonderful memories, from special times. I have even told Pop that I'm glad I didn't listen to him at the time, not in a disrespectful way mind you.

My mother Barb and I went through a phase in our lives where we didn't see that much of each other for months and months on end. My brothers will tell you that was probably a blessing in disguise as Barb and I crossed swords on many occasions, in a fun kind of way though. I think we were made of similar stuff although neither of us would be first to admit it. We had much the same sense of humour and would quite often have each other in tears of laughter, although she could also quite often be heard saying to Donna, 'I love him Donna, but I couldn't live with him,' or, 'Donna, take him home love, he's getting on my nerves now.'

I can't truthfully remember but maybe it was Barb who had encouraged me to join the navy in the first place. She certainly didn't attempt to talk me out of it once I had informed her and Pop of my career choice. 'Bon voyage,' they said. Charming! When I returned home on leave, her first question always seemed to be, 'How long are you home for, when are you going back?' The question was always delivered with a big smile on her face, I must add.

Barb, unlike Pop, did enjoy her football and although she was a Yorkshire lass from Hull, she would show more than a passing interest in how the Reds were doing – as well as the Blues, of course, so as not to upset my brothers. I used to take her to the odd game at Anfield, one of which was the last appearance of Ian Rush in a red shirt before he left for Juventus. She loved that day out with some of the boys and had a few beers in town and around the ground. Barb loved to laugh and she really enjoyed the banter with the lads. My younger brother Tony also took her to Goodison Park once or twice, but the look in her eye told me she didn't enjoy that as much!

In her heart of hearts she was a Tiger, a Hull City fan, and good on her. I really enjoyed watching the Arsenal v Hull FA Cup Final with her and Tony in 2014. From 2-0 up after just eight minutes, Hull went on to lose 3-2. It wasn't the best outcome but I still have a very fond memory of Barb sat there with a Hull City scarf around her neck that Tony had bought for her.

Your mother is the best friend that you will ever have in your life, bar none. Cherish her the best you can, for as long as you can. She is the one person who will stand by your side no matter what you do in life. We lost this amazing woman in January 2016 and it was completely unexpected. Fit as a butcher's dog, was Barb. She held down three part-time jobs well into her 70s and cycled every day but a massive heart attack took her in the middle of the night. I have often thought that your heart has only so many beats, so perhaps we should try not to use them all up too soon. Only 24 hours or so earlier the family were gathered together at a party for my sister-in-law Lesley's birthday. What really stood out for me from that evening was the fact that Barb was sat at her table eating olives, for the first time in her life. There's nothing unusual in that to a stranger but to those of us who knew Barb well, this was indeed completely unnatural for her. She was quite unadventurous with her food, very plain and simple seemed to satisfy her taste buds and yet here she was, voluntarily sampling exotic foreign fare.

I remember once, when all three of her boys still lived at home, devilishly we held her tight and force-fed her pasta. Pop was in fits of laughter. Pasta really shouldn't have seemed so foreign to her as she had been married to an Italian descendant for well over 50 years. Pop had tried to introduce this tasty dish to her on more than one occasion but had failed at every attempt. Looking back at that last meal together watching her eat her olives, I can't help but think that she knew something. Eating something alien to her, of her own free will! I haven't a clue how, but personally I think she knew.

I will remember until my dying day my last words to Barb as Donna and I helped her and Pop into a taxi that night, 'Goodnight Barb, love you loads.' 'Goodnight son, love you too,' she replied. How many of us are lucky enough to have had a conversation like that as your last words together?

Rest in peace mummy dear. If anyone ever deserves to, without doubt it is you! I miss her so much, every minute of every day.

I've met and sailed with many, many Scousers over the years and I got along with the vast majority of these boys and girls so well that I sincerely felt I had become one of their own. I have never felt anything to the contrary. Throughout my life I have come into contact with and built up so many relationships with these fine people. Even as I write this story there can't be many suburbs of Liverpool where I don't have relatives or friends living. My beautiful, amazing wife is an Anfield girl herself.

Getting back to the story after a big digression, I have never resembled – or ever will – these good people (wools) from taxi number three in appearance, so maybe I'm only half wool. They were decent enough folk; long-haired friends of Jesus, wearing scarves around the wrists, wouldn't harm a fly kind of people. This taxi was simply nicknamed the 'friends of Jesus' or 'Bible bus'.

Taxi number four was a sight to behold. Its inhabitants were, upon first appearance, the kind of lads you see most hours of every day. They were fully clobbered up with all the usual trendy street gear: Boss, Armani, Under Armour t-shirts, shorts, socks with flip-flops or sliders. Socks with sandals is a look I've never really understood and our forefathers took plenty of stick for sporting that appearance in bygone days. They were also all carrying small man bags around their necks – yet another popular accessory in today's fashion!

If ever you were unlucky enough to find yourself in the trenches (without an ex-serviceman that is) then these were the sort of boys you would want by your side. Dovecot boys, they played by their own rules. Leave them be and you would never have a problem with them; try and change their rules or cross them and God help you. I am not a religious man but seriously, God help you. Jamie later mentioned to me that when everyone had first arrived at The Arkles, taxi number four was the one he had wanted to be in. Its inhabitants, upon first appearance, appeared to be cut exactly from the same cloth as him, so I could see why he may have wanted to join them. Seats were allocated at the time of booking, however, so you sat where you had been allotted.

A line of thought I have always had is that you can learn a lot more about a man's character if you look deep into his eyes, more than you ever could just by listening to him.

Taxi number four was full of proper boys, with eyes that could break a man if so desired. I was grateful that these troops were going to be in our corner should anything unsavoury occur.

On the way home from the final, Jamie confessed to me that actually these boys were too heavy, even for him.

I would never have thought that Jamie was the kind of man to admit to something like that, he did know his limits after all, but he is now in his 40s.

Taxi number four was rapidly turned into a mobile pharmacy with varying substances on offer. Someone actually commented that 'even the wheels were made of lemo [cocaine]'.

If I am going to be completely honest, in my adult life it is no secret to those around me that I have enjoyed a smoke now and again. I would probably have enjoyed a smoke and a cuppa more than a few beers. But I'm now clean and have been for a long time. These warriors were carrying shit I'd never even heard of though; don't forget I was a sailor and a publican for numerous years and thought I'd seen and was aware of most things. The nickname given to this taxi was, quite aptly, the 'nutty bus'.

So there we were, four taxis with 34 people all attempting to travel almost 3,500 miles together by land and sea.

What could possibly go wrong?

8

The Leaving of Liverpool

THE CONVOY departed The Arkles at 6.30pm on Wednesday, 23 May. I must admit that I was quite emotional behind my sunglasses as I was leaving Donna behind. Do I really need to go? It's only a game. Can it really be worth leaving her for almost six days? It was so difficult waving goodbye to her out of the window, watching her stood on the corner of Stanley Park as the taxis pulled away. I'm not too big to admit it but there was a little tear that was starting to well up and I needed to disguise it from my new-found friends. I forgot to mention earlier that another reason this trip was a no go for Donna was the little matter of daughter number three having grandchild number eight any day. This also added to my feelings of guilt; I was going away and taking a chance of maybe not being home for the birth.

Donna and I have spent the odd occasion apart but after each time we have experienced it, we promised each other that we would try not to do it again. That's a big ask when you have five kids, nephews, nieces and brothers;

there are stag and hen dos aplenty and that's without any friend events.

That afternoon was a roller coaster of emotions for me. I was gutted that I was leaving Donna behind. She was the one who had convinced me that I had to go. She kept going on and on, telling me I couldn't miss this one. What a girl! I miss her when we are not in the same room. We have spent the vast majority of our relationship properly side by side – we work together, live together, sleep together. Even after all these years she still floats my boat.

It was going to be a long trip without the love of my life beside me. Donna is an Anfield girl from St Domingo Grove, is football-mad and has been on many trips at home and abroad following the Reds. She never has a problem with travelling by plane or train, or at least she endures them and never seems to moan.

I have often said to other people that when I met Donna it was the equivalent of being lucky enough to have won the lottery. She hates shopping, with a vengeance, be it for food or clothes, and loves her football. Donna is always first to put the football or the sports news on the telly. I enjoy the fact that you can have a proper conversation with her about the match and her knowledge of the Reds is second to none.

As often on these kinds of trips, the best and quickest way to introduce yourself and get to know people is the first shout of, 'Who wants a bevvy?' We weren't even out of Arkles Lane when those words were heard.

Up front we had the drivers Paul and Terry, in the back seats were the Carney brothers, and sandwiched in between were myself and Jamie. He sat next to me and almost as soon as the wheels had started turning, he lifted on to our seat something that can only be described as a small wheelie bin but without any wheels. I thought this was his holdall full of clobber, possibly all of his clothes and belongings for the upcoming trip. How wrong can you be?

Once opened up, this was in fact the biggest nose bag I have ever seen. 'How is he going to keep all that food fresh?' I thought. There was enough food for the whole trip, enough to cater for us all. I imagined Jamie to be around nine stone pissed wet through so surely this buffet was for all. But, for a great first indication of his character, Jamie just shouted out, 'Anyone want a sarnie?'

On our itinerary was to get down to Kent in order to catch the midnight ferry from Dover, or at least the 1am Thursday crossing. Then we planned to head across the Channel and turn left at France. Simple, or so it sounded.

Early on in the journey Jamie told us that he needed to get some presents for his kids; commendable some might say. Although later on in this story you will learn how his shopping habits differed from most people.

Jamie had desperately wanted to bring his eldest lad, also named Jamie, along on this epic journey. Just before we left The Arkles he mentioned that he could have got his lad a ticket at the last minute, but at that point no transport links were available. Not without a lotto win that is. Jamie hadn't realised that there was room in our taxi and once this came to light, he just proceeded to beat himself up even more.

The prices for flights to Kyiv were increasing by the minute. The operators were completely aware of people's needs and how desperate they were becoming in order to get to

Ukraine. As time was running out the prices weren't so much rising as spiking to obscene heights. I could just picture the tour operators' CEOs, sat there, smoking their Cuban cigars, sipping their cognac and champagne, rubbing their hands with glee at the prospect of selling more seats to good people who were desperate. Fat cats! Personally, I can think of a more fitting word than cats.

Eternal shame on them all, along with their partners in crime. The problem we have, you see, is there will always be someone willing to pay the extortionate fees and take your rightful place, and these people know it. They call it market demand; I call it complete and utter extortion.

The ordinary folk in the street need protecting from these kinds of vultures. But then I wonder just how many MPs out there may have vested interests in these kinds of companies? The Public Disclosure Act may well indeed throw up a few interesting names if one was to investigate and search a little deeper. I couldn't be arsed looking, however, as any findings would only serve to wind me up a little more, and there is not a lot anyone can do about it so why bother?

We could take a stand by staying at home and not paying the prices but such draconian acts of solidarity would only serve to vacate your seat for a tourist to sit in.

Jamie senior was proper gutted that his boy wasn't by his side; he mentioned this on more than one occasion during our trip.

I was in a very similar frame of mind as my sweetheart would have loved to have come along on a trip but via a different mode of transport. At one point when we were looking for flights, Donna and I felt so desperate that we decided to bite the bullet and were prepared to pay well over the top, just for a day trip. Then we found out they were sold out and no direct flights were available for a couple of days either side of the game. Literally the only option left available was a five-day trip via various planes and countries, with no bed involved as any non-flying time would have been spent at airports waiting for connecting flights.

Donna is the love of my life but she is definitely the last person I would want to be around if she is suffering from any sleep deprivation. She can be a proper nark if she doesn't get her eight hours a night. She knows it too but can't do anything about it so batting this option away was a no-brainer.

The time we had spent researching all options only served to hike the prices higher and higher. Even if we had managed to find a day trip, the cost involved was so high that if we had decided to pay the asking price it would have undoubtedly taken a huge shine off the occasion. How could anyone fully enjoy the experience after being three grand down for a day trip? Think about that – £3,000 for an in-and-out day trip including tickets and spends. I'm sure that even if the Reds had managed to bring Old Big Ears back home, the over-priced travel costs would have still stung for a long while after. It was a great privilege being there but it was still my hard-earned cash. At least Dick Turpin wore a mask!

On saying that, I know people would have happily paid a lot more to have witnessed the miracle of Istanbul.

The first leg from Liverpool to Dover seemed to pass quite quickly, and I can't remember anything out of the ordinary or of any significance happening on this shunt. It was more of a getting-to-know-you exercise, although two things do spring to mind.

One was that some numpty had turned up at the second pick-up point, The Rocket pub in Broadgreen at the bottom of the M62, without his passport. Tell me, how does that happen? Come on, it's possibly the biggest trip of your life and you turn up without the most important document you need (apart from the match ticket). I genuinely fear for some people. After the slight delay while his passport was collected, we started the taxis and our journey was about to commence in earnest. This time it really was wagons roll and Kyiv here we come. We finally departed the city at around seven o'clock that evening, which gave us five hours to join the rat race in the big dash south and make the midnight ferry at Dover. 'Big ask,' I thought to myself.

The other thing to note was that Jamie had emptied the complete contents of his wheelie bin before we had even got past Stoke on the M6 south. Point taken and proven time and time again – Jamie needed food, and lots of it.

We had only been on the road for about an hour and a half when we arrived at our first service station on the M6 for a toilet break. Jamie's shopping intentions were quickly realised almost as soon as we stretched our legs and without realising it at the time, this really was a sign of things to come. As we strolled out of the services, Jamie had no presents in his hands, just more food to keep his energy levels up. Interestingly, he had left his wallet back in the taxi!

It quickly became quite obvious to me that the nutty bus had a few similar characters to Jamie on board. I watched one lad walking across the car park back to his taxi with at least three two-litre plastic bottles of orange juice. He had helped himself to the juice in the service station shop and then ceremoniously poured it away down a grid. 'Why did you pour that away?' someone asked. 'Got no bogs on them taxis, need something to piss in,' came the swift reply.

That was about it on the road down south, just small talk and getting to know each other as we travelled on roads full of Redmen in various modes of transport, all heading on a temporary migration.

9

Leave With Ease

ONCE WE had reached the ferry port of Dover the scene in front of us was pretty dismal. It was wet, windy, cold and in the earliest hour of the Thursday morning. As I had expected, we were too late to catch the midnight sailing and we had only just arrived within minutes of the 1am check-in being closed. If we had missed this crossing it would have meant us all sitting and waiting around for at least another couple of hours until the next ferry.

The weather was awful in Dover and the thought of being stuck inside our taxis truly didn't appeal to any of us. We desperately wanted to get out and have a little walk around, stretch our legs on the boat.

The town was closed at that time of the morning, so there was absolutely nowhere to go and nothing to do. The place really was so uninviting. It actually crossed my mind at the time that if this was the first scene to greet me as I stepped off the ferry in the UK, then I think I would seriously consider turning around.

It's nothing personal but the port of Dover is not a very welcoming sight at all in my opinion. I don't know but maybe this is by design.

One thing I couldn't help but notice, and with great alarm, was just how easy it was to exit the UK. The four taxis had pulled up at the checkpoint booths just in front of the ferry, which was moored up at the dock. As departure was imminent, the boat was awaiting permission to close its doors and set sail. We pulled up to the passport control booths and our passports were handed in. After a few seconds of deliberation from the border guard, who carried on chatting to a colleague as she scanned the documents, her voice boomed out, 'Paul.' 'Here,' came the reply. And on it went, the names simply changing before each response of 'Here.' 'Terry.' 'Karl.' 'Jamie.' 'Stephen.' 'Another Paul.'

The border guard was, I would say, in her early 40s, and rather miserable I thought, but that could have been for any one of a million reasons. Maybe it was the hour of the day or even the weather. She took a quick glance into the taxi from where she was sat and without leaving her seat, handed our passports back to Terry. 'Have a good trip, bye,' she said, although her message was not really delivered with much sincerity.

I was almost rendered speechless as it went over and over in my head, was it really that simple to exit or even escape from the United Kingdom? All that was checked was our passports and the taxi's number plates. We could so easily have had another five or six passengers lying on the floor of our vehicle; there was absolutely no attempt to do a visual check or search the contents of the taxi whatsoever, or any of the taxis in our little convoy come to mention it. That was it, 34 people waved out of the country, it could so easily have been 50 or more. Trust me when I say that we could very easily have had at least another dozen or so troops scattered among our group, and it would have been easy to aid somebody on the run.

The nutty bus had nothing at all to worry about here. Their goodies were safe and sound and completely unchecked. The boys were probably gutted that they hadn't brought more with them, possibly to pass on to friends, if you get my drift. I'm not suggesting anything here, just guessing.

I swear that I have been through far tougher security checks getting into football grounds.

As we were late arrivals at the ferry port the place looked bleak and deserted, but once on board the boat it quickly became apparent that this vessel was rather full and most of the passengers were of the Liverpool Football Club persuasion.

A lively mix of Redmen. Young lads aplenty but also a fair gathering of supporters of all ages, both sexes and from all walks of life, with many differing styles. The vast majority, though, were of the socks and sliders brigade. The young bucks were out in force and it was a sight that put a big smile on my face. So many of our young local scallies were here and on the move. This is exactly what it used to be like.

Once on board the ferry full of Scousers, people were dispersing in all different directions. Some were off to the various bars dotted around the ship, some went to the restaurants to grab a bite to eat and some were doing a little shopping in the duty-free shop. Some were even looking for quiet corners to grab some shut-eye.

On the Channel crossing, Jamie was spending a little time with the boys from the nutty bus. Even though they were from different parts of the city he seemed to know most of these fellas, birds of a feather and all that! Their paths had crossed on more than one occasion following the Reds around.

Our drivers Paul and Terry were sleeping in the truckers' rest room and I think the brothers Carney were dining in the ship's restaurant. I was sat in a quiet corner on my own thinking about Donna; it sounds mushy I know but I could have quite easily turned around at that point. Seven hours in to my trip and I was already missing her like mad. How was I going to manage without her for six days? How was she coping without me? These questions just kept spinning around in my head until at some point I must have dozed off. The next thing I remember was the subtle bump of the ship's hull hitting the quayside, and we had arrived at Calais. The first leg was done and dusted.

As I gathered my senses, I couldn't help but notice the huge sense of excitement that seemed to grip the passengers as we docked. People were scampering around like thousands of red ants, in all directions trying to find their cars, vans, minibuses, coaches and can you believe, even motorhomes. If ever you get the chance to roam abroad to watch your team play then I urge anyone to at least think about that last mode of transport.

A motorhome and a proper bed wherever you stop. How luxurious does that sound? Plus you can take all your grub with you and even better is the idea of carrying all your clobber all pressed and hung up ready to go. Whatever mode of transport we had adopted, we all had one thing in common, we were en route in to Ukraine. Although it was approximately 2.30am there was a definite spring in most people's step. Even the boys from the old brigade, and I class myself as one, were positively lively. That buzz from first landing on foreign shores never leaves you.

For me, I think it would be time to pack it all in if that excitement were ever to fade.

10

Sunnier Climes

CALAIS: THIS is where we turn left. Another five border crossings and we'll be there.

Back on board the taxis with the wheels turning along the French roads, very much to my surprise I must have dozed off again. I slept on the short trips through France and Belgium as the next thing I remember was our taxi stopping at a McDonald's in the vicinity of Eindhoven in the southern Netherlands. We arrived there at around seven o'clock on the Thursday morning. It wasn't really a big kip but three and a half hours or so was good enough, especially after that little doze on the ferry. It was a lot more than I was expecting so I was quite pleased.

Within minutes of arriving at the restaurant, a sizeable queue was starting to form and snake its way out of the toilets. People were not only doing their business but were attempting to have the fastest strip wash possible. Brushing teeth and shaving only prolonged the process. I was determined not to be the last man in at this little convenience.

After a quick scan of the restaurant and being certain of no interruptions or embarrassment on either side I made my move, in to the ladies' WC. I wasn't alone in my actions, just the first.

All cleaned up and with breakfasts gathered, the troops were outside munching and enjoying the beautiful Dutch morning sunshine that had greeted us upon our arrival. There was a real buzz of excitement in the air as people were starting to realise that this was it. Our first day on foreign soil – no going back now, we were definitely on our way. We were in this together and it felt good.

Only half an hour or so into our breakfast break, a large bus turned in to the car park and came to a halt just behind where our taxis were parked. Maybe it's a natural reaction that's only attributed to travelling football fans, but if a bus full of troops pulls in to your vicinity, then your first thoughts are always that of friend or foe?

As the final was the last game of the season, we all knew there was a very good chance the bus could only be loaded with Redmen. It was carrying approximately 20 lads on board, some of whom were from our Wigan branch of supporters. They were a moody-looking team who looked like they could cause bother in an empty house. The usual sort, all in their socks and sliders. A team that you wouldn't really want to f**k with if you didn't have to, especially at that hour of the morning.

As these fine chaps disembarked from their coach one by one you couldn't help notice that one of them had recently had some cosmetic work done and had his nose rearranged, but not in a good way. Although he had attempted to clean up the mess there was a certain amount of evidence to suggest his plight was a painful one; the darkening of his eyes and a swollen nose was the giveaway. 'What's gone off there?' was the obvious question to ask him. 'Pissed off one of me mates on the way down,' was his reply. No more than two hours into their trip his friend had very kindly broken his nose for him. They had since kissed and made up though so all was well.

I've been on countless trips with these sorts of teams in the past. Now and in a more mature time in my life I feel it is time to let the young guns take centre stage. I'm more than happy to stay on the periphery these days and observe from afar. Sometimes I will even observe and reminisce.

After breakfast the taxi convoy rolled on, heading towards the west of Germany. This was where Jamie really began to start thinking of his offspring and acquiring presents from his holiday for them.

For some reason, stopping at service stations became more of must do and not so much of a need to. That wasn't an issue for most of us but how long was spent at them was becoming a major irritant, especially as far as one of our drivers, Three Amp, was concerned.

A little reminder that nicknames are just something that seems compulsory. On board the dad and lad taxi was another solo traveller who went by the name of Brad, a decent enough fella who spent a lot of time in the gym. Every single time the taxis stopped, Brad was first out with his shirt off. True, the weather was absolutely glorious for the whole trip, but Brad's obsession with the sun didn't go unnoticed.

'F**k me, I've seen more of his tits than me bird's,' remarked Three Amp. No disrespect was intended to Brad, but he quickly became known as Brad Tit. Simple and to the point; nicknames is what we do.

The time spent at these service stations just wound Three Amp up that little bit more, and it was becoming quite comical. However, the longevity of these stops was like music to Jamie's ears. He was like a pig in shit. Not only were presents from this trip on his agenda, at one point he mentioned to the lads that he was so far ahead he was even thinking about presents for Christmas too. We were still only in the last week of May; if that's not forward thinking I don't know what is!

The rate at which he had started accumulating his booty was quite alarming and possibly meant that we were in danger of overloading the taxi. If he were to keep up at this pace throughout the trip, then we were going to need to find more wheels for the return journey, or at least acquire a trailer. I'm certain Jamie would have taken care of that little issue if the need had arisen.

What a contrast of emotions; Three Amp raging the longer we remained at pit stops and Jamie grinning like a Cheshire cat, a boy on the make under the cover of 30 odd football fans. What could go wrong? He was in heaven. I nicknamed him 'Robin of Loxley'. Jamie was the nearest thing I've ever seen to this mythical being.

Another nickname suggested for him was the 'van pet', which was not in any way a derogatory term, just that he would wander off all the time and eventually people would start enquiring as to his whereabouts. 'Where the f***k has Jamie gone now?' or 'What's soft lad up to now?' In a caring sort of way, you might say.

Jamie was socialist in most senses of the word. I only say most because I had only known him for a few days and surely you can't get a true measure of someone in that time. Plus I doubt I know the true meaning of the word myself. Or even if socialism has ever been practised in reality. I'm not so certain it has.

Jamie needed his food, and also his sleep. When Jamie wasn't eating, shopping or having the odd drink he could be found sleeping like a new-born, but he really was a wise old fox. When Jamie wasn't involved in any of these activities he was on his phone – not playing games or any of that nonsense, but talking to his young family back home. After spending what seemed like an eternity on his phone he would turn and say, 'Can't wait to see me phone bill when I get back home!' 'Well, you're never off it,' I said. 'What do you expect?' 'It's all right for you c***s, I've got eight people I gotta talk to, I have to talk to all of 'em. Me bird's gonna do her nut when she gets the bill but it's her and the kids I'm calling,' was his defence.

On the journey from Liverpool down to Dover, Jamie had mentioned that he had lost both parents many years ago. Nothing too strange in that, you may think. A little further into the trip, his phone was up front by the driver being charged when it rang. Nothing too strange in that either. The strange thing was that as his phone was passed to the back of the taxi where he was sleeping, we noticed that his caller ID was 'Dad'!

'F**k me, it's me old man,' he said while rubbing his eyes.

He answered the call with the words 'All right, Dad' and duly carried on the conversation while the rest of us sat there silent and dumbfounded. The chat ended with 'See yer, Dad' and Jamie put his phone away. No one asked!

It turned out that Jamie had someone else in his phonebook listed as 'Dad', but you just had to be there.

11

This Ain't The F*****g Nürburgring

THREE AMP'S rages really were becoming funnier and funnier by the hour, although on more than one occasion I worried that he was heading for a heart attack. This boy really was getting closer and closer to the tipping point at every unwarranted pit stop, although these breaks weren't the only thing that was raising his blood pressure unnecessarily. Lots of things seemed to get to him and one particular incident really did warrant his angry reaction. At one stage we were tearing down an autobahn in the west of Germany at about 75 miles an hour when two of the taxis flew past us. You could say that their driving was a little reckless to the point where they almost appeared to be racing.

Porches, Mercs, Beamers and Audis were zipping all around us as if we were on the track at the Nürburgring, Germany's main motor racing circuit, plus the usual abundance of HGV wagons that needed to be negotiated along the way. This was one place where you needed all of your driving faculties with you, by the bucket load. It was not for the faint-hearted.

The two taxis in front really did appear to be taking unnecessary risks, all to gain a few extra minutes in our endeavour to reach our first night's destination in Wrocław. It was either that or a game of bravado between the two drivers, Terry (the owner) in the dad and lad bus and big Gary, who was possibly entertaining the nutty boys. Either way, it was madness. I have been driving professionally on and off for 35 years and these boys really did seem to be pushing it. They were either lunatics or just bad drivers.

I must add here though that all of the drivers employed for this trip did a fabulous job ultimately and got us to Kyiv and back home in one piece, so maybe they were racing, and damn good at it too.

Three Amp was becoming more and more irate by the second as this crazy exhibition unfolded before our very eyes. The next stupid manoeuvre from the taxis in front and boom, he was off, shouting and screaming, calling people every kind of expletive you can think of. His way of getting his point across was quite alarming.

Doing almost 80 miles an hour on a German motorway is one thing, but to pick up your mobile phone and have a proper rant at the lead taxi while doing so is quite insane, especially while trying to keep up for fear of getting left behind.

The western European countries seemed to be gone in a flash, possibly because of the driving tactics employed by the lads in their quest to be the first into Poland. The troops all clambered off the taxis and flooded into our first German service station. As such stations go, this one seemed quite posh. It had a restaurant that looked rather tidy and appeared to be one you would quite happily take your beloved to for a nice romantic meal. It was all Italian-looking with flowers and terracotta everywhere, and tables set, nothing at all like our service stations back home or anywhere else I'd seen on a motorway.

My first port of call was the toilet and upon my return I noticed Jamie wandering around the shop, casing the joint, scanning everywhere, checking for cameras and security. He was actually walking around inside the shop with a new baseball cap on. 'Jamie,' I said. 'The tag's still hanging out the back of that.' In Jamie's defence, he had only just woken up.

Upstairs on the landing by the toilets a formidable queue was starting to form, as two coaches full of German pensioners were on the move and had decided to call in to answer nature's call. They probably needed more pit stops than our own little convoy, someone remarked. Although Three Amp didn't think that was possible!

Can you believe it? Germans queuing! That was something I, nor any others in our party had ever witnessed before. Payback time, boys! The Germans were actually waiting in line to pay at a turnstile to gain entry in to the toilets. 'F**k this,' someone shouted and that was it. The boys were in, under the barriers and over the turnstiles.

I stood back taking a good look at the pensioners' reactions and the looks on their faces, wondering just what these indigenous people would make of us. Maybe they were wondering how we had won the wars, or maybe they completely understood! The looks on their faces really were quite comical. Payback with interest some might say. How ironic that these good people should queue when on home soil and yet totally disregard this practice when abroad.

After falling victim to their queuing practices, or lack of them, on many occasions while holidaying abroad, I found it quite difficult to show any sympathy towards them. A small part of me almost enjoyed it to be truthful. In fact, if their queue wasn't full of pensioners then I'm almost certain I would have pissed myself laughing. The last thing I wanted was to create a deluge.

Bizarrely, right next to this service station in the middle of nowhere was a sex shop. Well, to call it a shop is an understatement. This was massive and surely a distribution centre. My immediate thought was that Jamie and some of the boys would be off for a little nose around, and maybe a little shopping for their beloved. Not in the slightest; Jamie was more interested in the nutty bus, so off he went for a little socialising with his kindred spirits, and nobody showed any interest in the sex shop whatsoever. This was also something I had not witnessed before – a good team of boys totally ignoring a sex superstore when on our travels. I've seen this kind of shop getting swarmed over in the past in such places as Berlin, Amsterdam and a few other towns and cities across Europe. Wonders never cease!

After breakfast and what turned into another elongated stop, the taxis were refuelled, restocked with goodies and ready to roll on towards east Germany. Fed and watered, we were feeling good. We still had a hell of a long way to go before we could even think about Poland so this leg was definitely going to incorporate a few more stops at least.

The next couple of breaks were very much the same: shopping, eating, drinking, getting cleaned up and a lot more hanging around than was necessary. If you've seen one service station then you've seen them all, apart from the one with the posh restaurant that is.

After a couple more stops in the fatherland our convoy eventually crossed the border and rolled into Poland at around five o'clock on the Thursday afternoon, only two hours or so away from our digs in Wrocław. Much to Three Amp's annoyance once again, and after only 90 minutes or so on the road, the taxis pulled into yet another service station. Leaving him to rant at anyone who would listen, I was off to buy some liquid refreshments. After a quick scan around the booze aisle I thought, 'When in Rome,' so I bought some of the local brew at 16 zloty for a four-pack. 'Cheeky bastards,' I thought, although I then realised it was about £4, which wasn't bad for a service station I suppose.

After having a quick look around, Jamie decided he needed feeding before he could concentrate on any other activities he may have had in mind. He wandered off towards a cafe at the end of the building.

As Jamie entered, I followed him in just to have a look around more than anything else. Behind the counter I noticed something that looked very pink, turning slowly on the rotary spit. Whatever it was, it was dripping fat, and apart from looking vomit-inducing, it smelt disgusting too. A woman who looked like she had a good appetite but with a rather grumpy attitude appeared behind the counter and in a not so friendly voice barked at Jamie, 'What do you want?'

'Give us one of them, love,' he said to the charming lady as she fastened her apron. He pointed to the thing that was being grilled at the stake. 'Mate, you seriously going to eat that?' I asked. 'F****n' starving!' he replied.

I wandered out, leaving him to it. As I stood outside on that beautiful sunny afternoon, Jamie came and stood next to me beside our taxi, along with the takeaway that he had just purchased.

'Jamie, that's minging,' I said. 'Tastes nice,' he replied as he went in for his second bite. 'It f****n' stinks, get that thing away from me. It's still breathing, it's got a f****n' pulse,' I choked out, as I started to wretch. 'Yeah, I can taste the rubber off the car's tyres too, still nice though,' he said with a big smile on his face as he bit into it again.

I couldn't believe my eyes as I watched him devour his meal. At intervals in between chewing he would stop eating, examine its contents and duly discard any of the salad that was included in his kebab. 'Not eating any of that shite,' he would mumble to himself.

I walked off trying desperately to control my churning stomach. I would have seriously considered starving to death rather than put that thing anywhere near my mouth. I was once a chef in the navy and I swear Jamie's little snack didn't resemble anything I had ever cooked, or even witnessed being cooked before.

All four of the taxis were parked up in a row. All of the doors and windows were swung wide open, no doubt in an attempt at fumigation as these carriages had been abused on a rather large scale both inside and out over the previous couple of days. I suppose it's fair to assume that during their normal working life, taxis take a fair amount of abuse on a daily basis but I don't think these little carriages had ever suffered this much since coming into service. Some of the troops were just sitting around on the grass lawns chilling out. Others were inside the service station shopping but most were just enjoying yet another glorious early summer's day.

It wasn't too long into our latest stop when I noticed some young buck floating around, from a distance at first, but the more he assumed he was undetected the nearer he got towards our little convoy, creeping closer and closer until he was only a few feet away from our taxi. I couldn't believe just how brazen he was, or maybe he was a complete novice and only just learning his trade! There he was, having a good scan, casing the taxis. This kid was around 18 years old and was looking shifty. He had a lot to learn if he were to become a master of his trade in his chosen field. Who knows though, maybe it wasn't his choice? A desperate man is one who is probably the most dangerous of all and prepared to take a lot more chances than others would.

He definitely wasn't one of ours so I assumed he was a local. His eyes were everywhere, checking all around him, constantly looking one way then the other. From when he first appeared on the scene, I very quickly got on to him and a few looks, nods and winks between a few of our boys confirmed that I wasn't the only one to sense an intruder. This boy must have either been crazy or had balls of steel to even contemplate trying to get off with booty from 30 or so Scousers. He was messing with the wrong kind of people; our boys were well on top.

I feared for him as I considered the consequences of his possible actions. Luckily, I wasn't the only one to see this stray trying to immerse himself into the pack unnoticed. When I say luckily, I meant luckily for him. He soon realised that he was being watched from every angle, and his only way out was backwards.

This boy had nowhere to run if he made one wrong move. Unless he could fly, he would be trapped with consequences.

We were totally gobsmacked; this boy was completely out of his league. Any attempt at a snatch and he could have quite possibly and very easily become the next occupant of that cafe rotary spit. After hanging around for more than a few minutes the lad quickly realised he was way out of his depth, and as he eased his way back out towards safer ground he cast a glance in our direction as if to say, 'Fair enough, you win this one.'

He also left me with an astute awareness of my surroundings. We were in eastern Europe and these boys were made of different stuff. Persecuted and downtrodden for generations, the people there have a certain steel about them. They are tough cookies who take chances and play the high-risk game, quite simply because having nothing can make the rewards of the risk that much greater. The lad disappeared into the distance but you just knew for certain that he would be back to fight another day.

A question that kept nagging away in my head was, 'Were his actions derived from need or greed?' There I go, over-thinking things again. It doesn't do me any favours but I just can't help it.

12

Hotel Walton

WE EVENTUALLY arrived at our hotel in Wrocław at around 9pm on Thursday, 24 May, about 27 hours after leaving The Arkles. The area we were staying in appeared quite an affluent suburb of the city, situated in the west of Poland. As first impressions go I was pleasantly surprised as I am largely ignorant in my knowledge of Poland and assumed it was not one of the most developed European countries.

I had visited this beautiful nation once before on a stag weekend for my son-in-law, but that was to Kraków. To be honest, that wasn't much of a sightseeing trip. It was only bars and the odd strip joint that most feel are compulsory to visit on a stag do, although on one of the days half of the boys did go off to Auschwitz. Whether this was a short interlude from drinking or a culture trip, I wasn't sure; maybe a bit of both. A look into the history and its harrowing consequences would have traumatised me for days though so I didn't fancy that. I'd seen enough shit in my life and didn't fancy the idea of examining in detail any of those atrocities.

The other half of the group, which I was in, went off to watch FC Wisla Kraków in action on a freezing afternoon against Legia Warsaw, if I remember right. There wasn't one away fan in attendance and the most bizarre vision from this little experience was the one of a big team of riot police positioned in the away end. They were all kitted up in riot gear yet there wasn't a soul in this enclosure to protect. Maybe it was just their muster point for the game itself. With no away fans in attendance, I suppose the mobs of local muscle-bound skins were looking to vent their frustrations somewhere.

They were serious, wannabe old English football hooligans. These young local scallies were on to us big time, they didn't leave us alone and on more than one occasion they sought us out. A big thumbs-up to the old-time Wisla hooligans who, for whatever reason, did us proud and kept their young bucks at arm's length.

The old boys showed plenty of respect towards us but the young lads just couldn't get their heads around the fact that we were a party that consisted of both Reds and Blues together. They thought we should have been ripping each other apart, even on a stag do. I must admit that there was one very tense moment when things could have got really nasty as we were entering the stadium but these old fellas had quite clearly earned the respect that they commanded and clipped the wings of the young brigade and sent them on their way, thankfully.

After watching the first half and finding ourselves in this precarious position, we decided that in order to maintain our safety and wellbeing it would be wise to try and negotiate our way out of the stadium before the second half started. I'm sure the old boys would have maintained their support for us but the numbers were well stacked in favour of the young scallies. Still, it's another experience. It made Millwall away seem like a walk in the park, which it has been every time I've been there.

If Poland isn't skint then why else would its people disperse around Europe and beyond looking for gainful employment? Perhaps, like everywhere else I imagine, there is money around, but only in the hands of the few. The cost of living in their homeland is a mere percentage of what it is in western Europe. The cheap cost of living means low wages, therefore some leave and work abroad for a decent pay packet, then send the money home. This enables their families to become fairly affluent or at least upper working class, therefore ensuring a good and comfortable lifestyle upon their return. If and when they do decide to return home, that is. They seem a lot more willing to make short-term sacrifices in order to gain in the long term. Good luck to them.

Admittedly, Brits have been working abroad for many a year, but these Poles and their eastern European cousins seem to do it in much greater numbers.

When I called our digs a hotel, I was being kind with my words. I meant it looked very nice and inviting from the outside; it was quite a big building and appeared almost modern upon first impressions. It had a decent plot of land attached with a great view across the fields. This gaff would probably cost well over a million pounds back home but step inside, and don't forget to wipe your feet on the way out! It can only be described as Walton Prison from back home, although that's not a place I've experienced myself.

What a shit hole! Bunk beds with mattresses that were so thin, no memory foam here, just memories, and bad ones at that. Some rooms had three beds, some four, some five and so on but all were well below the usual standard you would expect in this modern era. Damp and cold, most of the rooms, or should I say dormitories, had no windows either. Is it not a basic human right to see daylight?

My immediate thought was to get cleaned up and get out, see the local sights and down a few scoops so I wouldn't have to think too much about our abode when we got back. What else was I supposed to do? This place wasn't comforting in the slightest. There would be prison riots on a daily basis back home if these were the kind of conditions that the inmates had to endure. The only difference here was the fact that we could walk out and down a few beers before returning and crashing out for the night in our cells. A sort of open prison!

Three Amp decided he wasn't going to sleep in Hotel Walton and chose to sleep in our taxi instead. The couple who were in one of the other taxis also opted against the hotel that night and kipped in one of the vehicles. I couldn't blame them.

There's no way on earth that I would have even contemplated asking Donna to bed down in something so decrepit and unkempt as this place. I also doubt she would have been impressed if I had suggested to her that we sleep in a cab. It would have been off to town to find a better residence for the night. We have both served our time travelling across Europe, sleeping in train stations, airports and even pub lounges, but we are both getting on a bit in life now, so I think we deserve a little more comfort these days.

Around 20 of the boys were up for a little wander into town to take in the sights and sample the delights. The two brothers, Jamie and I were soon in the queue for the one and only shower that was in our penthouse block on the west wing. In order to use it you had to hold it with one hand and soap yourself with the other as it was hanging off the wall. You also needed to run around in it to get wet. You also had to be careful where you stood within the shower enclosure. This place was disgusting.

An hour or so later we were all booted, suited and ready to go see the local sights. Big Gary, the driver of the nutty bus, was nipping into town for a pizza and alcohol for the lads who had opted to stay in. The journey had been exhausting for some but others wanted to carry on the fun or even start having fun. Cue our taxi and 15 minutes later, we were in the centre of this old Polish city.

Once we had arrived in the centre of Wrocław we couldn't help but notice the beauty of the place. History just poured from every building; at times you really got a sense of how things might have been during those dark days of the war, when the Germans were marching through and terrorising most of Europe along the way.

In most, if not all towns and cities across the globe there will be a main square, usually next to a town hall, a parliament building or something of the like. Wrocław's was typical in that it was surrounded with an array of bars, restaurants and shops. Situated around the perimeter were the usual high street names you see in almost every city, everywhere you go.

You will always find an Irish bar. These watering holes are usually a little more expensive than the other localised establishments offering their wares. On football trips, though, you will always find them packed with Scousers. Maybe because it's a big part of their heritage I suppose, as Liverpool was once dubbed the capital of Ireland.

In the 1840s an estimated one and a half million Irish migrants had come to the city, fleeing their homes because of the great potato famine and disease back home. Almost 20 per cent of the entire country's population had crossed the Irish Sea looking to start a new life in America, but a lot of them had stayed in Liverpool.

With the Scots coming down in their numbers and the Welsh on their doorstep, Liverpool was – and still is – a very Celtic city. With our Viking friends invading a little earlier than our Irish arrivals, along with our Chinese neighbours living in the oldest Chinese enclave in Europe, this city is diverse and welcoming. Liverpool is very much a cosmopolitan city with our roots coming from all corners of the globe.

For those who don't know, Liverpudlians have the Vikings to thank for our nickname. When invading Liverpool, they brought a tasty dish known as Lapskaus with them, which became known locally as Lobscous – essentially a beef stew. The locals could not afford the lob or beef part of the dish so mainly ate only Scous. According to accounts our forefathers ate the veggie option of this dish in copious amounts and thereafter became known as Scousers. Every day is a school day!

There was plenty of noise emanating from the Irish boozer we found in Wrocław, mostly Liverpool songs that inevitably drew us in. Once inside we found that it was indeed full of Reds supporters all enjoying themselves. Lots of songs, lots of laughing and lots of pats on the back. Handshakes, nods and winks from people you had not encountered for a while. That old indigenous thing rearing its head once again.

Supporters of clubs lucky enough to play in Europe will identify with that warm feeling you get when you first walk into a boozer abroad and familiar faces are all over the place. You get a nice sense of being a part of, and belonging to a big family.

After what must have taken half an hour or so making my way through the crowds and saying hello to people I hadn't seen for a while, I finally made it to the bar. 'Seven pints of Tyskie please,' I asked politely. 'Twenty-six zloty,' the barman replied. Holding my fingers up, I said again, 'Seven pints, please.'

'Yes, I know, 26 zloty thank you,' he repeated with a smile. 'Oh, okay, thanks.' I quickly gave him 30 zloty and told him to keep the change. I was convinced he'd got his sums wrong.

I grabbed myself a tray to carry the beers outside to the boys and placed them on the table. They were all enjoying the night, just chilling and watching the world go by. It really was a beautiful setting and the atmosphere around the place was a very pleasant one.

'How much was that, Ste?' came the question. 'Just over a fiver,' I answered. Well, anyone would have thought I had fired a starting pistol at the Olympic 100m final as the scramble to get up to the bar was rapid. 'Relax boys, we got ourselves a 24-hour bar here,' I told them.

The next round was seven pints, two Bacardis and two packets of ciggies, all for less than £10! 'This is going to be another long one,' I thought to myself, with a little smile on my face as I settled down to enjoy a couple of ice-cold beers.

After plenty of drinks, laughter and socialising with people from back home, some of the younger members of our travelling army had decided to have a break from all the singing and joviality inside. They began to gather outside next to us, in the bar's decking area. The young bucks soon realised that Wrocław was a magnet for American students and there were plenty of them knocking about. These students were witnessing first-hand the drinking habits of travelling European football fans. Many of them had strayed into the bar we were occupying, simply because they were curious as to what all the noise and excitement was about. The young Americans were in awe and many of them said they had never witnessed anything like it before and were only too keen to lap it up and enjoy the occasion. There appeared to be plenty of them mingling with the Redmen and everyone was in great spirits. The American students were in their element and the young Scousers gave the impression that were having a ball too. I sat once again reminiscing about the good old days when I was one of them.

After maybe an hour or so sat outside, everyone was getting along famously with no sign of trouble whatsoever when two Polish policemen strolled up and stood by the bar. They stopped for a minute or two and spoke discreetly to each other, whispering into each other's ear as they looked around the seating area. After respectful smiles all round from the lads, there were nods of acknowledgement from both parties, or so I thought.

What happened next was quite shocking, sobering, and a big reality check. As the policemen started to walk away, one of them turned around and stood there with his middle finger extended in our direction. Then in a voice that was intended to be heard, he said, 'F*****g learn to speak Polish!'

The remark was aggressively aimed in our direction as he spat on the floor without ever losing eye contact with our group. A little reminder of where we were, you could say.

'Dobry wieczor i powitanie [good evening and welcome] to you too, sir,' I thought.

The Polish plod were out to make a statement, or at least these individual members of the local constabulary certainly were. 'Just don't, under any circumstances react, boys, that's what they are after, it's what they want,' I thought nervously to myself.

A gentle reminder to anyone reading: don't even think about overstepping the mark here, or in any other place that is still trying to catch up with the civilised world. Their draconian attitude still rules, with a big iron fist. We are not liked or wanted in these countries.

I find this attitude really short-sighted. The boost the travelling hordes must contribute to the local economy would surely outweigh any silliness that comes with it.

It is a fact, that in all of Liverpool's forays into Europe in 2017/18, there hadn't been one single fan arrested. I reiterate that in all of my experiences following the Reds around, Scousers have never been hooligans for the sake of it. You are always going to get some idiot kicking off, but that happens every weekend in every town and city all over the world.

It's also true though that the boys from the Anfield Road End and even the early Kopites could mix it with the best of them if required. They could and would defend their pride with honour and with frightening consequences if the need arose. But, in all the years travelling around with the Reds I can honestly say I've not once seen someone kick off just to make a name for themselves. Sure, I've seen lots of incidents down the years that have been cringeworthy and sometimes over the top, but never unprovoked. Some Scousers may be scallies, chancers and on the make, but never hooligans, vandals or any of that nonsense that the national team seemed to attract.

Don't get me wrong, Scousers are no angels and it is true that both Liverpool and Everton have got more than their fair share of proper nasty bastards among their numbers. But I have never witnessed the smashing up of public property, pubs or town centres just for the pure hell of it.

If there was a big incident going on somewhere, you would probably find the Scousers some distance away around a corner. They would be perusing what's around while the police are engaged elsewhere, if you get my meaning.

While we are on that note, sadly I must say that you will very rarely find a Liverpool fan at an England game, well not the Scouse Red anyway. There are very few flags of St George flying around this city when England are involved in any tournaments.

One reason for this is most likely due to the Irish heritage in the city; there can't be many Scousers knocking around without Irish blood in them somewhere along the line. Another big reason for this is the legacy left behind from Margaret Thatcher's Britain. Liverpool people, or at least the city's football fans, simply don't associate themselves with the English national side anymore.

Liverpool was left to rot in 1980s England. Downing Street gave us the distinct impression that it wasn't just willing to cut this great city off from the rest of the country, it wanted to cut us off and let us drift away into the Irish Sea.

On the back of this, it also took the British governments of any persuasion almost three decades to finally face up to its responsibilities and give people the tools and finance required to bring justice for our lost souls and their families from the Hillsborough disaster in 1989.

Is it any wonder we have little or no feelings at all when it comes to being nationalistic towards England? The Kop even has songs proclaiming to be Scouse, not English. We have flags, banners and t-shirts that say the same, a sort of 'Scousalonia', relating to the dispute between the region of Catalonia and the Spanish government.

And as a club we have been vilified for decades by opposing supporters domestically, both at home and away. The songs and chants are always the same, calling us 'murderers' in relation to the Heysel disaster, saying we robbed and pissed on the dying and dead at Heysel and Hillsborough, that Hillsborough was our own fault and we're 'always the victim'. You get the gist.

Who are England playing? Will they win or lose? We couldn't give a shit either way. Even if we have any of our own club players representing the English national team, the only thing we are interested in is that they all come back uninjured. I don't speak for all but I know for a fact that I echo the sentiments of many.

How ironic is it that we now get vilified for not supporting our country's team? Some people have very short memories, not to mention the double standards displayed. Folk want to have it all ways, I suppose. I speak as an ex-England fan who once did support the national team at home and abroad back in the early 1980s.

After a few more rounds sat outside the bar, it was time to hit the taxi rank and head back to Walton-In-Wrocław. The problem we had was that opposite the taxi rank was a totty bar. Jamie turned and said to me, 'Make f****n' sure I stay out of there.' 'With yer, bud,' I replied in total agreement.

These kinds of establishments have never done anything for me; I always preferred the chase back in my day. In your face, so to speak, wasn't the way I played the game. In fact, back when I was younger, I used to chase the married girls. Well, I wouldn't say chase as that sounds a bit pervy. I was more subtle than that and would possibly dangle a few carrots, you could say. The bigger the rock on her finger, the bigger the challenge.

Before you start mudslinging in my direction and judging me, ask yourself who was the bad guy, them or me? After all, I was the single one. If these ladies weren't happy at home, then how was that my fault? Yes, it's true that I wouldn't like it to happen to me, but if it were to happen then the first person I would question would be myself. My conscience is clear as far as I'm concerned, although some would like to see me burnt at the stake. I can understand that.

Although I can't remember the exact details, we somehow never got to the taxi rank as planned. We ended up in another bar practically next door to the Irish one we had spent the last couple of hours in. We seemed to go round the square in circles, if that makes sense. As the hours of the night, or early morning I should say, were gently drifting by, the good-time hawkers were coming out to play. They were in their numbers outside our bar, baying the lads, trying to entice some of them back down towards their dancing club around the corner. We spotted some of the nutty bus crew across the road entering the venue. After a few moments of contemplation, Jamie was hot on their tails.

Not for a second did I think he was after some form of entertainment; I assumed he was more likely to be after some of the other things the boys may have had in their possession. I'm guessing this of course, but I don't know. Either way, wanting to keep my word and save my new mate, I went straight in after him. I was immediately stopped at the door by what looked like a huge female wrestler. Shit! You wouldn't pick a scrap with this one. If she said jump you would simply ask how high.

The scene must have appeared quite funny to anybody watching on. Jamie was trying to get through by explaining that he just wanted to talk to his mates, and therefore he wasn't going to pay an entrance fee, while there I was, trying to wrestle him back by his arm or any other part of his body I could grab hold of in a frantic attempt at getting him out. Ducking and diving along the way as I was trying my best to avoid 'Krystyna the killer' knocking me clean out. There was a three-way argument going on between us, all at the same time.

As this pantomime unfolded the nutty boys were completely unaware of our predicament. They were deep inside the bowels of this entertainment complex, enjoying themselves, at extortionate prices no doubt, although money didn't seem to be an issue for these boys.

I eventually somehow managed to get Jamie out of there, thankfully without feeling the might of Krystyna's right hook. This time it was straight up the stairwell as fast as I could persuade Jamie to move up on to the street to find a cab. The excitement and efforts of such an eventful day and night must have caught up with me as I sat in the back of our ride back to our hotel.

I can't remember too much after the taxi had started to pull away. My radar was still on as I was checking out landmarks but anything else was a bit of a blur. I can't remember any conversations with Jamie or the driver taking place. When I awoke the following morning, I was fully clothed and on top of my so-called bed. Exactly how I had planned it.

As I gathered my senses my immediate thought was, 'Did I manage to get Jamie back with me?' A blurred glance across our dormitory, scanning the beds and their occupants, confirmed that I had. He was in the top bunk opposite me above Karl's bed. Job done. Don't you just love it when a plan comes together?

The Polish prison was starting to come to life far too early for some of its inmates. 'Shut the f**k up!' 'F****n' shut it!' 'I'll choke you f*****s out if you don't wrap up!' 'Noisy c***s!' 'I'll f****n' bang you clean out if you don't shut it!' These were just a few of the nicer comments being shouted out and echoing across the corridors of Hotel Walton early that morning.

A couple of the lads mentioned that while waiting in line for their morning shower they had noticed some mice scampering across the dining table. A quick reminder of our dwellings as if it were needed. This place had so much potential but it was almost criminal the state it was in.

Myself and a few of the lads decided to jump into one of the taxis and head for the nearest McDonald's, again. The queues were extraordinarily large for a Friday morning, I thought, without knowing how big their queues were normally. I only really had the lines back home to compare with, apart from brief visits to the ones in Holland, Belgium and Germany. I decided to give it a miss and wait outside.

As I was leaving the restaurant, Three Amp shouted to me, 'Ste, have you ordered yet?' 'Can't be arsed, mate, not waiting in that queue,' I shouted back. 'Forget the queuing lad; order it on one of them big self-service tablets,' he said. These things weren't tablets; they were those big standalone things. It looked like two of them huge widescreen TVs placed on top of each other. I had certainly not come across these before. What a dinosaur!

'No good with them computers bud, I haven't got a scooby,' I told him. 'Come ere, I'll show yer!' Within seconds Three Amp was whizzing through page after page of the menu. He sure knew his way round these tablets. I ended up with a cheese and mushroom toastie in front of me, washed down with fresh orange juice and a coffee. He was good; I didn't know McDonald's even did toasties!

It was Friday morning, the day before the game. Back at Hotel Walton people were starting to surface, come to their senses and get organised in readiness for the penultimate leg of our journey. One of the funny things to witness that morning, as we prepared to leave, was that a lot of the troops were relieving the hotelier of his possession of pillows. These items were being borrowed to make the onward journey a little more comfortable for all. Basil Fawltski was soon on to this little pilfering and he was quickly on his toes scanning the taxis one by one, looking for anything that he may have mislaid. No sooner had he collected the pillows from one taxi than its stock had been replenished within seconds. The poor guy was kept running around in circles until eventually the taxis started their engines and pulled away. I estimated that he had lost maybe 20 per cent of his bedding that morning, if that's what it could be called. Some of the lads insisted it was a fair deal because of the sub-standard accommodation he had offered. I don't think we paid more than a fiver each so maybe it was a bit tough on the bloke.

In another 24 hours or so, all being well, we would be in Shevchenko Square, Kyiv. Plans had been made in abundance with everyone to meet with friends and families who were all converging on this beautiful city.

13

Memories Of Old Kyiv

I HAD in fact visited Kyiv back in 2001 to watch Liverpool play against Dynamo Kyiv, but I don't recall the place being so inviting back then. It was boys only on that trip and as we wandered around from bar to bar, it didn't take long to notice that someone had been assigned to follow us and watch our every move. This person, who could only have been described as a KGB sort of character, was hiding in doorways. He was concealed inside a long overcoat with his collar up and topped off with a trilby, while lighting a cigarette. Very stereotypical, just like the movies. He was following our every step, as we sampled the local hospitality but he really was shit at playing hide and seek; his attempt at being incognito was so comical that every time we were preparing to move on, one of the boys would go out and tell him so. How things change, and I'm not just talking about landscapes but police measures too. Back in 2001, I was probably one of no more than 500 Redmen, who were mainly Scousers.

I remember vividly the morning of the game on that first trip to Kyiv. The scene that unfolded was hilarious. After breakfast, people were attempting to leave the hotel to have a look around and explore the city by daylight. They wanted to go stretch their legs and walk their breakfasts and hangovers off. The boys were leaving the hotel lobby only to find that all LFC fans were under hotel arrest. This was for our own safety, we were reliably informed by the local plod and army. Apparently, Dynamo had among their number a rather large group of 'Ultras' who were keen to enhance their reputation on the European stage.

Within an hour, the hotel we were staying in was completely ring-fenced by the authorities. They were all dressed in complete riot gear, batons, shields, helmets and with a few canine companions. Just how crazy were these Kyiv Ultras if this was the peace-keeping force? After giving it a few moments' thought, one of our intrepid explorers had started to nose around inside our new-found prison. Within a few minutes he had managed to find an escape route out through the hotel's underground kitchen.

The hotel's chefs were quite amused watching a hundred or so Scousers moving out in an orderly single file through their kitchen, all smiles and nods of appreciation. Half an hour after the hotel had been placed in lockdown by the authorities, it really was quite amusing to witness the scenes of chaos from afar. The realisation hit the Kyiv plod that the hotel they were guarding was, in fact, almost empty.

Once we had made our escape, we went on to enjoy a lazy day, nice and quiet, in one or two of the welcoming bars dotted around the city. Later that evening, the authorities were not very happy to see more than a few Scousers strolling up to the ground only an hour or so before kick-off, unescorted and in a jovial mood. They seemed to panic a little until some bright spark must have realised that all the numbers were now accounted for and they quickly ushered us into the stadium.

14

Bristol Beauts

WE LEFT Wrocław around midday and much to our surprise the two vacant seats on our taxi had been filled. There was no mention of this whatsoever from Terry, the owner, but then why should he tell us? He was out to make dollars and earn a living, the same as the rest of us. A little heads-up wouldn't have gone amiss though. These two blokes from Bristol had flown into Poland and we were taking them along with us to Kyiv. Ash, who was in his 20s, and Lee seemed okay, but myself and the other lads couldn't help but notice there was a strange kind of bond going on.

Lee, who was in his 50s, was cut from the same cloth as Brad Tit from the dad and lad taxi. Although a polar opposite in the bodywork department, he too removed his top at every opportunity. We couldn't help but notice that he had one of his nipples pierced, with a pink bar through it. Not that there's anything wrong with that at all and I'm not judging here but it's not what we are used to seeing on a football trip with the local lads. Maybe it's a Bristol thing; all I can say is that it stood out, literally!

What also stood out was how big these fellas were. Let's just say they took up most of the bench seat that I was perched on.

They were not big in a hammering the gym kind of way but they displayed more of a good-living physique, if I was being kind with my words. Me being me, I got inquisitive; work, married, kids, home life sort of questions. I wasn't being nosey but just trying to find a basis for conversation. Their replies were vague to say the least so I didn't interrogate them much further. I was only trying to make conversation and strike up a relationship as we were going to be sat next to each other for the next day or two. It seemed polite.

Lee said they had picked up the bus because they loved the crack and being a part of the atmosphere. He explained that he had experienced some of the best times of his life travelling abroad with Scousers. Sorry, they were nice enough blokes, but neither of them brought much to the party. I'm not knocking them but to say you love the crack and a giggle and sit there and say very little for two days, wow! If I'm not mistaken, I think their only contribution to the party of any sorts was to offer a few bottles of beer around when they first got in the vehicle. They only really spoke when spoken to. I did get the impression though that both boys had enjoyed their time in our taxi. Maybe that's what was meant when Lee said they enjoyed the banter. They enjoyed watching what shenanigans people got up to. Fair enough if that's the case.

With an extra two people on board, this also meant that I had lost my bed. These boys were on my perch. Jamie, on the other hand, had long since found a more comfortable abode in the back of the taxi. He was sleeping on top of everyone's holdalls along with the food and booze in the luggage compartment, so he wasn't too affected by their arrival at all.

Jamie could do everything in abundance. I later found out that, like me, he was not a big drinker, although he could eat and sleep for Britain. At one pit stop I went around to the back of the taxi, opened up the tailgate to let him out and there he was, actually sleeping upside down. Just how is that possible? This became Jamie's bedroom of choice. To be fair to him, he did on more than one occasion offer to swap places with anyone who fancied using his bedroom for a bit to stretch out. His offer was always conditional though, usually by the way of a sexual favour. I don't think Jamie was too surprised to find that he got no takers, and I don't think he was too disappointed either.

Cheers Jamie, but that boot full of bags and supplies didn't look that comfortable or inviting. Nice thought though.

Sometimes on these long trips you can find yourself needing a toilet break with no pit stop ahead for miles. At one point I was bursting and had no option but to use an empty bottle. The size of the two Bristol beauts sat next to me meant that it was extremely difficult to hit the target. My concentration was taken up by trying not to hit my fellow passengers as much as it was hitting the bottle. Those baby wipes really do come in handy.

The taxis pulled out of Wrocław as if we were a marching army invading foreign lands, not in an aggressive way, more of being proud and in solidarity. After an hour or so driving past miles and miles of fields, Jamie was unusually awake.

He had spotted an old lady by the side of the road selling her wares and suggested that we should turn around and go back to buy some ice creams off her.

'No way Jay, you can't go back and have her off,' Terry said sternly. 'Would never dream of it mate, I support them little shop and business owners all day. I'd give her the money for an ice cream but wouldn't take it. I would even give her a tip. It's the big corporate c***s I have off,' stated Robin of Loxley!

A little further up the road, Jamie was surprisingly still awake. A conversation took place that at the time made absolutely no sense whatsoever, on any level, on any scale. It still doesn't to this day.

Jamie mentioned that he was so fed up listening to the news as it was always bad, and suggested that someone ought to invent a good news show. 'What sort of news are you thinking about mate?' asked Paul. 'Not sure, maybe news about a young kid who lost both his feet!' 'How on earth is that good news?' I asked, dumbfounded. 'Well, there's a company that does transplants,' he replied. 'Same question Jay, how is that good news?' came the next baffled enquiry. 'He got to walk again,' said Jamie, stone-face. 'Oh yeah, get it,' Terry delivered in a sarcastic tone. 'And where would you get the donors, Jay?' asked Three Amp. 'If there wasn't any at home then I'd import them from Africa or somewhere.' 'What! You would import feet from Africa?' everyone asked in disbelief. 'Yeah, it could work!' said Jamie. 'And what if there was little demand?' stammered Karl, from behind his tears of laughter. 'I'd just have to make wellies out of the feet,' Jamie replied seriously and with a straight face once more.

Three Amp had no option but to pull over as he couldn't drive because of the pain brought on by his laughter. Everyone was in tears, doubled over, all apart from Jamie that is. He was sat there, poker-faced as he tried to figure out the flaws in his idea.

This was in no way a racist conversation on any level, just complete and utter nonsensical dialogue where someone was trying to make logic out of something completely and utterly illogical.

Then again, maybe that's how the socks and sliders trend began in the first place!

15

Don't Buy *The S*n*

THE NEXT stop was solely for the purpose of a toilet break. I'm not sure if that was the original plan but it turned out that was our only option anyway. We rolled into a place that was deserted and had long since been used for any commercial purpose. It was just a run-down building with a huge plot of land that was once possibly a truck stop. If we had called into this place at night then I'm certain not many of the troops would have left the taxis, no matter how desperate they were. It would have been plastic bottles at the ready.

The place looked so uninviting and moody, so no wonder it was empty. This was the sort of area you could easily imagine a horror movie being filmed. As it was another beautiful summer's day, these thoughts quickly evaporated from my mind. Three Amp appeared rather relaxed as even he knew we couldn't possibly spend that much time there. A toilet break was all this place could ever be.

The only other visitor was one of those huge American juggernauts that spends weeks and months on end out on the open road. The ones that have their living quarters in their cabs right behind them. There was also a smaller rigid wagon parked up but this motor almost looked abandoned. There was absolutely nothing for Jamie here, and nothing for anyone more to the point; no shopping, no eating. Jamie wandered off and nobody really took any notice of his disappearance until it was time to hit the road once more. After a couple of shouts of, 'Jay, Jamie,' he reappeared with a huge smile on his face and nodded towards the juggernaut. 'I wonder what's amused him here,' I thought. I strolled across the car park for a closer inspection and the evidence was there for all to see. The big American truck had been covered in 'Don't buy *The S*n*' and 'Total Eclipse of *The S*n*' stickers!

This is a campaign that has been running for some time in an attempt to halt *The S*n* being distributed and sold on Merseyside and beyond, in the aftermath of the Hillsborough tragedy, all thanks to someone named Kelvin Mackenzie and his bare-faced lies just to sell a few extra copies of his newspaper. He was that rag's editor at the time.

His printed version of events about that fateful day devastated the families and friends of victims beyond belief, as well as those of us in attendance that day, who were unfortunate enough to witness the tragedy unfold. The newspaper's stories were completely damning towards the whole of Merseyside.

An independent inquiry led by a truly wonderful man named Professor Phil Scraton proved beyond all doubt that this devastating tragedy was in no way the fault of any Liverpool supporters. Sadly, these findings didn't finally exonerate our fans for almost three decades. But even after

Professor Scraton's findings, *The S*n*'s apology was diluted to say the least. Too little, too late.

The 'Don't buy *The S*n*' campaign has been running quite successfully for many years now and these little stickers are very much in evidence at most, if not all Liverpool games, home and away. I have also witnessed them being displayed all around the world and you wouldn't believe some of the obscure places they pop up. They have been seen in Las Vegas and outside the Vatican to name just two.

Jamie just has to be doing something in his waking hours. Like him, I bore easily and need to be active most of the time. I'm so restless that I find it difficult to sit and read a newspaper.

Placing the stickers around this big American truck had amused him somewhat, for now at least. To be honest, the rest of us enjoyed it too.

16

The Greatest Man I Ever Met

I FEEL this is the ideal place and a perfect opportunity for me to express a personal thank you. I know I am not alone in expressing my sincere gratitude, for which this fine gentleman is so deserving.

Professor Philip Scraton is a critical criminologist, academic and author. He was heavily involved in the Hillsborough Independent Panel and was the head of research. I have only had the good fortune to have met him once in my life. Never before have I felt such a need to thank someone. The urge was almost overwhelming. I just had to approach this great man.

It was at a game at Anfield that our paths crossed for the one and only time. I noticed that Professor Scraton was stood in the reception area of the Main Stand and he was like a magnet to me, in the most respectful way. I wasn't seeking guidance or anything of the sort. I only needed to shake his hand and offer my profound thanks. That was the only thing on my mind.

Professor Scraton was extremely receptive and a conversation began that lasted for no more than five minutes.

Looking back, it was a very emotional time for me but it was such an honour just to be in his company. There are simply not enough superlatives to express how I felt meeting him. Thankful, respectful, grateful, I was so in awe.

After only a few minutes with him I began to feel a weight lifting from my shoulders, having been hanging over me for so long. I can't say that this weight was a permanent fixture and so heavy that I couldn't function normally. What I can say is that it was and still is there, always lurking in the background and never too far away. Some days are good, some not so good. After a few wise words from Professor Scraton. I wouldn't or couldn't say that he was a faith healer that afternoon, but something was definitely hitting home, I felt different. How can a five-minute conversation have such a profound effect on someone? I just wished it hadn't taken 30 years to get there.

What this colossus of a man must have gone through in the quest to extract justice, I can only imagine. Sifting through around 450,000 documents took more than three years, before delivering the findings. Just how strong does a person need to be to do that? I'm not so sure I could have done it. In fact, I know full well that I wouldn't have even managed to get past the first page.

I have been extraordinarily fortunate in my life to have met some great and wonderful people; footballers, sports stars, actors, celebrities, singers, politicians, people from all four corners of the globe and from many different walks of life. In fact, normal everyday people are often the most wonderful. I must say though, that without any shadow of doubt, for me it is Professor Scraton who tops the lot.

Professor, I for one, will be forever in your debt sir. You are a true hero, in the very highest sense of the word.

Professor Scraton turned down a knighthood from the establishment on moral grounds. In my opinion, for what it's worth, he has more morals in his little finger than every one of the establishment put together. I called him sir out of an earned respect, not as a result of a gong given out by the elitists.

A lot of people are deserving of their title but there are far more who aren't. He wasn't alone in his endeavours and a huge debt of gratitude goes to all by his side. Those amazing people worked so tirelessly for so long.

I have not and never would claim victim status after attending the game that day in Sheffield. I was there and have had to live with it like so many others.

I travelled to Hillsborough that fateful day on a coach full of the usual faces, all in fine spirits and looking forward to watching the Reds book our place in yet another Wembley final. Another possible Merseyside final at Anfield South was on the cards so there was a little more excitement than usual.

Travelling on our coach that day were two lads who never got to come home with us. Two seats were to remain empty on our harrowing journey back home across the Pennines.

James Delaney was a young buck just starting out on his adventures. I think James was attending his first big away game. Jimmy Hennessy, on the other hand, was old school and had been going the game for a long time. A proper fella and a cool dude to boot. A real Mod, he had a Lambretta scooter and all the gear. Jimmy was popular with most of the lads and he was never short of ladies flashing their eyelashes at him either. I knew Jimmy from many previous trips and also the local boozers back home.

I survived on that horrific afternoon. Somebody's hand was surely guiding me along with my old mate Gary Sheridan. We were both pulled up into the West Stand, above and away from the Leppings Lane Terrace minutes before the fatal crush.

One question has burned away inside my head for many years. 'Why me, why did I survive when so many women and children didn't?' Fate may have been with Gary and I on that day but the guilt of survival remains forever. We had both attended the exact same fixture the year before, the FA Cup semi-final against Forest. Same venue, similar scenario, but in the 1988 meeting, the authorities had closed the Leppings Lane tunnel moments before Liverpool fans entered. This meant the supporters just naturally migrated towards the side entrances to the terraces with no problems.

On 15 April 1989, the tunnel was left open and fans streamed into the tunnel in their hundreds.

Such a simple operation of shutting a gate could, and would have prevented so much pain and suffering for so many.

My pain can only be a fraction of what other suffering souls have had to endure for so long. I think of you most days. All of you.

Later in the evening after meeting Professor Scraton, when I was sat at home with Donna, I began relaying my experience of the conversation. While explaining my feelings to her, I felt the quickest rush of emotion I had ever felt in my life. It hit me like a bolt of lightning; one second I was fine and chatting away, then the next second I simply crumbled into Donna's arms and sobbed uncontrollably.

17

200 Yards In Five Hours

GETTING BACK to the tale of my trip, it was time to roll out and head for the Poland/Ukraine border crossing. It was approximately 12 hours away, with a little detour into Kraków airport to pick up the wife of one of the lads off the Bible bus. She had flown in that morning to meet the taxis.

Stupidly, I was half looking out for Donna and then wishing we had been more thorough with our research. Maybe she could have done this stretch, but then maybe not. My head was spinning again.

Many thousands of fans were travelling to Kyiv using so many different options. It was really interesting trying to map out the routes in that people had endured. It appeared as if every major city in Europe had Redmen departing from its airports. They were leaving from any UK airport just to get on to the continent, landing who knows where and then joining the dots until eventually touching down somewhere near to Kyiv. It never fails to amaze me the lengths our fans will go to. Our real home-bred fans, that is. Fair enough, our tourist supporters clock up the air miles between them, but how much research and effort do they actually put in to get to watch the Reds? More often than not, theirs is a package trip with everything organised for them.

For our indigenous supporter, the main concern is getting from A to B, then B to C and so on. They will get there eventually. They always have and always will. It's more than a tick off the bucket list for them.

After we had picked up this young lady from the airport, the taxis remained stationary. Once more, nobody knew the reason why so Three Amp was off complaining again, and Brad was out showing his tits again, it was like *Groundhog Day*.

The taxis started rolling after about an hour, and we were excitedly informed that we should be at the border before 10pm. We were only on the road for an hour or so when for some reason unknown to us at the time, we detoured off the main motorway heading out of Poland and took an A-road towards Ukraine. We passed through lots of quaint small towns and villages on our diversion and eventually came across what could only be described as being like Operation Stack, which is when the Dover port back home is having difficulties with the ferries for whatever reason.

In this instance, the authorities order all HGV wagons to park on the M20 in Kent heading towards Dover. Three lanes consisting of hundreds of vehicles are all parked up going nowhere for the foreseeable.

Terry had decided to piss off the other travellers parked up. He just put his foot down and whizzed through the bus lane straight up to the border crossing barriers. The convoy then had to follow seeing as Terry had the paperwork for all four taxis. The queue we had just jumped must have been at least three miles long. People who had been stranded there for hours, if not longer, appeared to be taking a great deal of interest in us, and not in a nice and friendly way. This could have quickly turned into a very nasty incident if we were not too careful.

Crowds were gathering to listen to anything the border guards had to say to us. One of Terry's employees back home was a Polish lad and he became our interpreter over the phone. In the next few hours this bloke was to become invaluable to us. I haven't a scooby as to what was being said but judging by the border guard's expression, our contact from back home seemed to be getting through to him, attempting to make things as smooth as possible. Our interpreter's words appeared to do the job because after some loud directions from the Polish authorities, the gathering crowds begrudgingly and slowly began to disperse and return to their own vehicles. Although not being fluent in Polish, the comments shouted in our direction didn't sound very complimentary at all.

We were all told in no uncertain terms by our Polish friend back home to be polite, smile, speak when spoken to and avoid eye contact wherever possible. We had also been advised on how to offer bribes to the border guards, hidden in passports. This, we were informed, could possibly make our crossing a little easier. As we were sat there waiting, I could sense that people were getting a little anxious.

The main man on the Polish side of the border looked like some baddie from a James Bond movie. A big f****r, he looked super fit and as disciplined as they come. This fella was made out of granite. I wouldn't have fought him but I bet the women loved him.

Surprisingly, looks can deceive, even in these scenarios, and it turned out that he was actually quite chilled, but one of his understudies was just the opposite. He was a weedy little t**t whose look resembled that of Simon Pegg, the actor, only a couple of stone lighter and not even slightly comical. He was the sort who was probably bullied at school and this was his dream job.

As old chiselled jaw opened up the first passport he spotted the €10 bribe and remarked, 'Money is not so important to us here in Poland, maybe to the Ukrainians, but not to us here.' He then let the €10 note slip from the passport and on to the taxi floor. At this point the tension was almost unbearable and the next few minutes seemed like an hour as he carried on examining the passports with his stern face.

Little Simon Peggski, however, was really getting the hump. All fidgety and jumpy, he wasn't very happy at all. I'm not sure if it was because he had missed the chance to make a couple of Euros, or simply because of the attempted bribe.

These people are very strict on cars and vehicles leaving Poland and all documentation must be in place. No paperwork, no excuses, you're not getting through, or at least the vehicle isn't.

By all means you are welcome to walk through their borders, if you have your passport that is, but if your vehicle documentation isn't in order then you've got big problems.

It turned out that although we had four taxis, we only had three V5 documents. One of the log books was missing. This revelation not only added to the tension but delayed us even further.

From the minute we had arrived at the checkpoints, until finally clearing the borders hours later, at no point was I ever confident that we would be allowed to proceed. Five hours of complete uncertainty can take a lot out of a person. Passports handed in, checked, given back, phone calls aplenty, passports retaken, checked again, given back again. Every time a phone call was made our passports were taken and checked again, and again, and again.

All through this I couldn't help but wonder where the nutty boys had stashed their goodies. These lads had nerves of steel and surely bollocks made of the stuff to even contemplate carrying whatever shit they had through this kind of border. 'He who dares, wins,' they say.

The Polish authorities wanted to impound the taxi without its V5. Of all the vehicles, it had to be ours, the other three were good to go. It had crossed my mind that maybe the missing V5 was a godsend for the nutty bus simply because more attention was drawn to our vehicle and therefore not as much to theirs. Everything happens for a reason, eh!

After what seemed an eternity, we were finally given the all-clear to proceed through their border. Thankfully, our Polish friend back home had worked some kind of magic and managed to get us through without the required documentation. Poland behind us, the Ukrainian border was 200 yards ahead.

The Polish border control seemed quite modern with their techniques, phone calls, computers and the like. The Ukrainians, on the other hand, were something completely different. There appeared nothing modern about this checkpoint. It was like stepping back in time. As we drove very slowly across the short divide that separated the two countries, we could see a small army of soldiers armed to the teeth. They had teams of dogs all wearing muzzles – big, nasty-looking dogs. It was reminiscent of a scene from some old concentration camp movie. Once again, we had been advised to drop a cheeky €10 into the passports as they were handed over for inspection.

Our taxi was the second in line. The first official to approach us was a woman dressed in an army uniform, who I'd say was in her mid-50s. She opened the first passport, noticed the money, smiled and shook her head. Then in the same way chiselled jaw had done back at the Polish border, she just let the cash fall from the passport on to the taxi floor. The female officer never uttered a word and at this point the tension was becoming almost unbearable once again.

A policeman then approached our taxi to aid his colleague and he also proceeded to check our passports. It was at this point that the Ukrainians got a little bit jumpy. The problem was that Three Amp's passport photo was in no way any resemblance to how he appeared on the trip. He was quickly off on one, insisting it was him in the photo, but they were having none of it.

He was taken from the taxi and escorted to an office, completely surrounded by robocops and their not so friendly looking canines.

Quite comically, on his way you could hear his plea of, 'I'm a Sagittarius, born on a Saturday. Here's all my other kinds of ID. I've got my gas bill, my phone bill, council tax,' as his voice faded away into the distance heading into their little office. What have I said about servicemen being organised,

*Jamie's Juggernaut, Pre- Don't buy the S** decorations*

Outside the Irish bar in Wroclaw, with the Carney brothers

Should be a doddle!

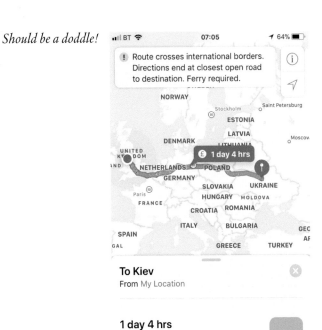

What more do you need?

Arrival in Kiev. Myself, Jamie, the Carneys and two of the lads off the 'dad and lad' taxi

The 'May' family. Uncle Jamie with bro Terry and his boys in Shevchenko Park (Dad's picture held up)

Karl Carney enjoying the party in the park

The Dortmund bus that Jamie had shown great interest in

Myself, Jamie and the Carney bros just before kick-off

Drivers Three Amp and Terry, Jamie and myself outside the Westfalenstadion. Home of Borussia Dortmund

European royalty meet again, this time in Kyiv

Paul and Karl ready with their flag, for the biggest stage of all as the atmosphere builds

Even the police cadets were out in force

Karl inside his living room and his bedroom, all cleaned up after his sandstorm ordeal

Mixing with Dynamo Kyiv fans

How did Jamie get his hands on 'Old Big Ears'?

prepared for anything? Three Amp had every kind of ID you could think of with him.

The other big noticeable difference between the Polish and Ukrainian borders was the fact that on the Ukrainian side, they appeared to have a lot more female soldiers staffing their frontier. This fact didn't go unnoticed, mainly by our servicemen on board, and these fellas were drooling. 'How is it that all these birds look so fit?' one of them remarked. Their uniforms looked fitted, made to measure and credit where it's due, they did appear to wear them well. It's funny how all three servicemen commented on how 'feminine' they looked, when our ladies in the forces back home are 'made to dress like f****g men'. Their words, not mine.

When Three Amp finally returned to the taxi after being carted off by the authorities, he was surprisingly grinning from ear to ear. It turned out that he'd been interrogated by three of these women!

Three Amp said his charm had got him through. This was a surprise to us all as none of us realised he had any! Whatever it was, we were grateful as all four taxis were through, although we did have a little more drama regarding the V5 once again with the Ukrainians.

Three Amp later laughed with us when he admitted that he actually looked nothing like his passport photo. He said he looked more like he'd eaten the person from his passport a long time ago.

We were through and as soon as the barrier was up, we were away. Over five hours to travel 200 yards.

Before we left the border, I turned to Terry and asked out of curiosity, 'How come we took a detour earlier, mate, why didn't we just carry on following the signs? Wasn't there a border crossing on the main motorway?' His casual reply was, 'We diverted because the motorway borders are tougher, the one we just used is one of the more lenient crossings!'

He got this little heads up from his Polish employee back home. We could still have been at the other one today.

18

Welcome To Ukraine

TERRY HAD arranged another Hotel Walton sort of residence for the night ahead and we had planned to be at our destination by 10pm on the Friday. A one-night stay in the city of Lviv would give the drivers the chance to rest up more than anything else. This is the country's second largest city after Kyiv and most of us we were quite looking forward to our first night of Ukrainian hospitality.

Because of all the drama with the border crossings we had not got through the controls until well after 1am on the Saturday. As it was the day of the game, it would have been pointless to check into a hotel for only a couple of hours. Kyiv was still 500 miles and almost seven hours of driving away. We would only have had three or four hours' kip before we needed to be on the move again. That's without any local beer time.

The vote was cast; we decided to forget the hotel and call into somewhere that was brightly lit. Maybe a hotel car park or a service station, anywhere that appeared safe really, just to park up and use to get a few hours of shut-eye.

Once we had left the borders behind, we were almost immediately driving through a small town. This was another place that looked moody. Although it was the wee small hours of the morning, there were small pockets of people standing around on street corners. They were all staring, straining their necks trying to peer into the taxis with a pleading sort of look on their faces. It was almost like a scene from *Village of the Damned* or some other zombie movie. Foot down; let's get out of here. These unfortunate souls gave you the distinct impression that they would have had your gold teeth out as you laughed with them.

We drove on looking for sanctuary, a safe haven for the next couple of hours, but we ended up in a disused petrol station possibly a mile or so down the road from the town of the living dead. Three Amp, Terry and all the other drivers of the taxis were running on empty; they were completely shattered. They desperately needed to rest.

A quick look around found that the only other vehicle that was parked up was an articulated lorry. The occupant was sound asleep and the curtains on his cab were closed as he had clocked off for the night. Jamie's eyes lit up briefly but like the rest of us, the day's excitement had taken its toll. It was off to sleep for all, or at least trying to.

Three of the taxis were in agreement to stay but the nutty bus had different ideas. They wanted to hit Kyiv as soon as possible and one of their drivers, big Gary, was only too willing to help. None of us were aware at the time but the nutty bus was having electrical problems. They had no air conditioning, no phone charger points, no radio, and basically no electrics. It would have been tricky if it had started to rain. The starter motor was apparently sticking and their windows kept steaming up with condensation. As a result of the conditions on board their taxi, the windows weren't the only thing getting steamed up. Understandably so, I thought. Don't forget that taxi number four was loaded with serious naughty boys. To compound the issue, the vehicle also needed a bump start after each and every time it was parked up and turned off.

There was no doubt in my mind that any one of these bad boys could have bump-started the vehicle on their own, but that wasn't the point.

The point was that Terry and his travelling mechanic were starting to piss these lads off, big time, with excuse after excuse, and apparently pretty lame ones too. Big Gary was raging the most as he was livid and threatened to knock both Terry and his mechanic clean out. After the brief altercation between Gary and Terry, the nutty bus was pushed into working order and the troops were gone. 'Let's get to Kyiv before this heap of shite stops completely,' someone shouted as they sped off into the night. Best of luck lads, hope to see you in town later.

Thinking back to when we set off from The Arkles, I did wonder at the time how their taxi would cope! It was 14 years old and didn't really look up to the job of a 3,500-mile round trip in the space of six days.

We had a few hours to try and get some shut-eye, and I do mean try, as it was practically impossible. Jamie was in his usual luggage compartment, so without a doubt he had the best bed for the night.

Eight fellas taking turns, coughing, sneezing, farting and snoring, all in a confined space, rendered it impossible for me. Trying to sleep sat upright only compounded the issue, plus the fact that the area we were in appeared dodgy to say the least. Surely it made sense to have somebody acting as a look-out. Maybe it was only me that was a little wary of our surroundings. It's probably a habit from my navy days. When visiting lots of towns all over the Americas, you quickly learn to never let your guard down.

It was about 5.30am when the other taxis started to show any sign of life. Doors opening, people were stepping out and viewing the glorious Ukrainian sunrise. Considering the lack of sleep, and certainly the lack of quality sleep, I would have expected a lot of good people to be feeling a little grumpy that morning. Surprisingly most, if not all appeared to be in fine spirits. The most probable reason for this was the fact that the day of the Champions League Final was here. We were only 500 miles and seven hours away. Only!

If anything can shatter the illusion of that beautiful early summer's morning watching the sun rise above the horizon, it must be the sight of 30 or so fellas brushing their teeth and having a piss at the same time lined up against their taxis. I felt embarrassed for our female travelling companions. If they did manage to avert their eyes then surely the sound of cascading water, and lots of it, would have been impossible not to hear. With an enormous amount of beer consumption in the previous 50-odd hours, most were pissing like a racehorse. Apologies, ladies.

On the next part of our journey, the policing methods we were to expect now we had entered the Ukraine quickly became clear. Every time we stopped, the local plod were all over us. Even without our unscheduled pit stops we were pulled over on numerous occasions and questioned as to our business, as if it wasn't obvious. Every time we had a pull, the officers of the law would ask a few questions, have a look at our passports, then take a photograph of the taxis' number plates. After this routine repeating itself a couple of times further into our journey, we realised that the tactic the police were using was to take a photo of our number plates with their phone and text it on to their next county's legal department.

Initially four taxis had entered their country, but only three were now in convoy. The local plod and their national colleagues were highly suspicious and very nervous. It was as if they expecting a throng of thousands of 1980s English football hooligans.

We had to explain each and every time we were pulled over that taxi number four had gone on ahead. The police were thorough and menacing, albeit with primitive means. We just never felt welcome, anywhere.

Further into our journey, we pulled into yet another service station, where I witnessed one of the funniest episodes I have ever seen while travelling to a game.

If you've never seen or driven on Ukrainian motorways, then I can tell you that their hard shoulders are the polar opposite to ours back home. Theirs consist of approximately two feet of tarmac and the rest is either a hard or soft verge. As the weather was red hot and had been for a while, most of the land appeared parched and dusty.

We rolled into a pit stop that was basically a wooden shack with an actual huge dust bowl for a car park. There were a few articulated lorries parked up but there was no one about. A little bit eerie I would say, not the sort of place you would visit if you didn't need to, and definitely not if you were on your own. This theme appeared to be a regular occurrence in this part of the world. Admittedly the closer we got to Kyiv itself, the more civilised the places to stop appeared to be.

The three taxis rolled in and were all parked in a straight line, one behind the other. People were off the taxis and answering the call of nature, having a smoke or just stretching their legs. Brad was out of his taxi showing his tits once again. After only ten minutes or so the troops starting climbing back on board. We could smell Kyiv and wanted to taste it as soon as possible.

I was standing by the side door to our taxi, talking to the Carney brothers. Paul and Karl had their backs to the road facing me. I assume a wagon or something of that size had brushed the hard shoulder back along the motorway because out of nowhere came the biggest and fastest dust cloud I had ever seen in my life. It reminded me of a scene from some war-ravaged Middle Eastern territory.

This thing was furious and silently heading our way. I turned towards the taxi, jumped aboard and slammed the door closed behind me. It must have been a self-preservation thing; my automatic pilot just switched on and I was on my heels, gone. My excuse was that I was thinking about the greater good. Our taxi had its entire contents, passengers, drivers and all of our belongings on board. Myself and the brothers were the only ones on the outside. If the door had remained open then the entire taxi would have been completely covered, both inside and out with thick dust.

Paul and Karl had disappeared; the noise of the sandstorm hitting our taxi had drowned out any screams that we may have heard. These two fine men, two brothers, so cool and so sharp, were locked out of the taxi. They had no alternative but to stay put, covering their eyes, their mouths and their ears. In fact, every orifice you can think of. Sit tight, take what was coming to them and ride it out.

After what seemed an eternity but in reality was just a few seconds, this dusty twister had rapidly battered the taxis and disappeared as quickly as it had arrived. Once the storm had subsided the picture that emerged will stay with me forever. What remained was three taxis absolutely covered in dust, and lots of it, and these two boys standing statuesque. It was reminiscent of those people you see every weekend on most city high streets, pretending to be a statue, painted bronze. A future career there for you as street artists, lads. I was the first with my hand in my pocket looking to throw a little loose change into their hat. Priceless, that one.

The pretty boys didn't seem so pretty just then. After plenty of abuse hurled in my direction from Paul and Karl, they eventually appeared to see the funny side, but nowhere near as much as we had done. We moved out of the dust bowl with the brothers calling me all the shit houses under the sun; they were filthy, covered in thick dust from head to toe. As I said, it was for the greater good.

About an hour or so from Kyiv, we surprisingly had another pit stop but in fairness it was to allow everyone to freshen up for the final march into town, especially the dust victims. Quick showers all round, a last round of drinks and off we went on our ultimate leg.

We arrived at Kyiv around 1pm on Saturday, 26 May. The day of the game, a full 66 hours and six border crossings since leaving The Arkles.

Job done, and a huge thank you to Paul, Terry and all the other drivers. I'm sure these fellas would more than hold their own in the Dakar Rally.

19

Shevchenko Park

AS OUR convoy rolled in to Kyiv around lunchtime, we found Shevchenko Park, the official fan park allocated for Liverpool supporters. It was named after the poet Taras and not the footballer Andriy. The weather was a very respectable 27°C.

We asked the local plod, who were out in force, where we could park the taxis, 'Just park here,' one of the officers replied. 'What, next to Shevvy park?' Terry asked. 'Yes, park there,' he said sternly. This is very convenient, we all thought.

The park was at the very bottom of the E40 carriageway that ran straight into town. This meant that we could be on the road and out of there in a flash if required. The park itself, although being a decent space that you would enjoy strolling around in, was a lot smaller than I had anticipated, and indeed a lot smaller than what was required, especially at the epicentre where the stage had been set up, surrounded by pop-up bars and eateries. Had the local authorities really done their homework and looked into how many Liverpool fans were expected? It was going to be interesting to watch how this small parcel of land was going to cope with thousands upon thousands of Redmen lapping up the sunshine, all singing and dancing, and drinking gallons of booze that appeared to be almost free, in relation to what we pay back home anyway.

The really pleasing thing for me was the fact that there were so many Scousers around. It was heart-warming to hear lots of Scouse conversations going on all around us in Kyiv. It was wonderful to see so many of the old faces coming out to play and by the way, some were really old.

Ukraine has a closed currency thing going on. You can't take the country's money in and you can't bring it out. I don't know how this affects the economy, but this place made Poland seem quite expensive.

The shops and off-licences that surrounded the park had queues that went on forever. There could well have been more fans queuing for beer at the shops than actually in the park itself, and the park was heaving. The warmer weather encouraged more consumption of alcohol.

The party in the park really was in full swing. The stage in the middle had the popular Scouse band Cast belting out some tunes, along with another local hero, Jamie Webster.

Could things really have got any better? They could have done if Donna was with me. I missed her.

Events were starting to get a bit too lively for me so I motioned to Jamie that I was making my way out to the periphery of the park and he closely followed behind. The park wall looked a good bet so off I went, treading over hundreds if not thousands of empty beer cans and bottles along the way.

'This is going to be some clean-up operation,' I thought, as I managed to escape the mayhem.

We just made it out as the idiots started launching beer through the air; our timing couldn't have been any better. I have mentioned that I am a more mature fella these days, or even old you could say. I have experienced lots of things but I can never remember wanting to get soaked through with beer before.

You have the one set of clobber on which has got to last you the whole day and night and some idiots start throwing jugs of beer around for a laugh, albeit plastic jugs I must add.

If these people want to behave this way, then good luck to them, I'm always happy enough to watch from a safe and dry distance.

This is not a Scouse thing. The beer-throwing exercise is apparently a Stoke City phenomenon which has since caught on at many major events. I can't get my head round that one. Why on earth would anyone want to do that?

'I'll never understand you kids today!' Pop would often say. That day you sincerely hoped would never arrive had done – the day you start sounding and thinking exactly like your parents.

Jamie and I decided to move away from this bedlam, and I also needed to get down to the ground to pick up my match ticket. Although I had the promise of a ticket, it wasn't yet in my possession so in that situation there is always a nagging doubt in the back of your mind. You are always uncertain and extremely anxious until it is in your arse pocket, safe and sound.

We had been midway through Poland when I unexpectedly received a call. 'Is that Stephen?' a voice on the other end of

the line enquired. 'Speaking, who is this?' I asked. 'This is ***
here, *** told me to call you, there will be a ticket waiting for
you at the stadium,' came the reply. 'That's amazing, I can't
thank you enough, thank you so, so much,' I replied like an
excited child who had all his birthdays come at once. 'You're
more than welcome, Stephen, enjoy the game, bye!' And just
like that my ticket was confirmed. As I said earlier, I never
will reveal the names of the people involved in making that
happen but I am eternally indebted to them.

The call set me off on another rollercoaster of emotions,
feeling completely thrilled to bits and yet utterly dejected at
the same time. Another massive pang of guilt struck when the
call I had just answered revealed that a ticket for my beloved
was also on offer too. I really wanted my best mate with me.
I so wished Donna was beside me, sharing my emotions and
experiences. My head was all over the place but at the same
time I knew Donna would be thrilled to bits for me.

It was only a short walk from the park down to the
Olimpiyskiy National Sports Complex so Jamie and I set off
enjoying the finest ambience a man can find, a football man
anyway. After every turn of a corner you were greeted by
thousands more Redmen; the whole of Liverpool appeared
to be here. The atmosphere was so intoxicating that alcohol
wasn't really necessary. We enjoyed the slow stroll down to
the stadium, taking in party after party along the city centre
streets. These had wisely been turned into pedestrian-only
areas for this event.

The local entrepreneurs had taken advantage of this and
had set up street bars and food stalls. They also wanted to
get their hands on a slice of the cake that was to be shared

among the city's more permanent establishments. The bars were rammed full for most of the afternoon and into the early evening. It was like one huge street party. It must have felt like a lottery win for all the local businesses in this beautiful city. Very best of luck to them I say, and they were the perfect hosts, much more welcoming than on my first visit almost 17 years earlier.

Most of the parties seemed to have a face or two I knew among them, which only served to make my smile wider and wider as the afternoon progressed. After meeting my contact and collecting my ticket from the stadium, I turned to walk away thrilled to bits that I finally had a ticket and then the realisation hit me; €140 face value, €280 if your partner goes with you. Want to take your kids? Forget it! Believe it or not, my ticket was in the third-lowest-priced category. Yet another example of capitalism being off the scale. Why can't we all make a little instead of the few making a lot?

Sorry, I'm ranting again!

With my ticket firmly in my back pocket, we decided to make our way slowly back up towards Shevvy Park. Jamie had been in contact with his older brother, also called Terry, who was in town with his two teenage sons, Aaron and Elliot. They had all arranged to meet up back in the park. That's a big ask I thought, like trying to find a needle in a haystack up there.

En route, Jamie decided he needed to answer the call of nature. He went into a bar to find a toilet and as I waited outside, I took full advantage of the temporary outlet this bar had set up on the pavement in front. Very clever, I thought to myself. 'Chotyry pinty [four pints] please,' I asked the barman.

'Thank you, that's 100 hryvnia [Ukrainian currency].' 'Cheers mate, have a good day,' I replied, handing him the money. 'Good luck to your team,' he remarked with a smile on his face. A decent sort!

Jamie reappeared and I handed him his two pints. 'About 50 pence each them, Jay, this is a giveaway,' I told him. Beers in hand, we continued along the high street towards the park, taking in this incredible buzz that was all around us. As is the norm on these huge footballing occasions, the pre-match atmosphere on the day of the game and even the night before is often better than on the main event itself. People are filled with expectation and as such the mood is one of excitement and belief.

As we took our time strolling along, enjoying every second of what was happening all around us, we were approached by two Australian blokes wearing Liverpool shirts. They latched on to us, asking about the price of beer, where to get it, what's the local brew like etc. Whenever I am away from home, I always like to try the local brews, sample the culture and even try to learn a little of their lingo.

By making a little effort with their native tongue, you'd be surprised to hear how many doors that has opened for me over the years. Respect, politeness and effort can get you so far in this life, and get you in to a lot of places too. I learnt that a long time ago and have reaped the rewards ever since.

I offered one of the Aussie lads a local beer to taste. After a big gulp, he told us it tasted like piss and the look on his face confirmed his dislike of the Ukrainian brew. After composing himself, he then stated that he needed to find a proper drink. 'Don't tell me you've come all this way to drink Castlemaine

XXXX?' I said with a hint of sarcasm in my voice. 'That's piss as well mate, I'm looking for Foster's,' came the reply. These two were exactly like the tourist supporters I mentioned earlier. Could you believe that this, a major European final, was their very first game?

I don't blame these fellas; it had cost them thousands of pounds to be there. What did piss me off, though, was when I attempted to start a conversation with them regarding how many Scousers in relation to tourists were actually in town. 'It's great to see,' I commented. 'Yeah, all your houses will be getting burgled back home now,' came the reply! What a f*****g beaut! Spends top dollar, travels halfway around the world, wants to be a proper Red and his first conversation is the same old stereotypical piece of shite that we've been hearing for decades. 'What did you just say?' I said and before he had time to gargle out any kind of reasonable explanation I continued, 'You best f**k off, knobhead!' I wasn't the only one upset by his comment and I noticed Jamie was sizing him up ready to pounce if he had decided to continue with his insults. The Aussie attempted to laugh it off and make a few more of the same tired old jokes. He got no second chance as him and his mate were once again firmly told to 'jog on'.

Australians gone, we headed back to the park. Jamie was quite rightly desperate to catch up with his brother. Terry had been settled in town for four days along with his two sons, and had the city well mapped out. We later learned that Terry had actually been weighing up the possibility of buying the city centre apartment he had been renting. It would have cost him £10,000, but 18 months' rent and he would have his money back.

'I know our kid's near; I can sense him,' Jamie said on more than one occasion. As we wandered around for a little while, we were again stepping over empty cans and bottles in their thousands everywhere we walked. The bins provided by the authorities were never going to cope with this little recycling job. They were overflowing almost as soon as the park had opened to the travelling Kopites. I didn't envy those responsible for this clean-up operation.

'I know he's close,' Jamie kept saying. After no more than five minutes looking for his family amid this giant sea of red, suddenly a slightly older fella leapt straight into Jamie's arms. 'I knew he was near,' Jamie said to me. 'I just knew it!'

There was a real tear-jerking moment in what happened next. A family picture was requested and as Jamie, Terry and the two young lads posed, Terry went into his small man bag and produced a photo of their dad to hold up for the photo. Jamie said, 'I think I'll call me old fella now,' as he lifted the picture up to the skies.

The three of us were chatting and having a beer soon afterwards, when I mentioned to Terry that Jamie was on the phone earlier during the trip to their dad. A knowing smile appeared on both their faces but again, there was no explanation.

As brothers go, I got the impression that Jamie was the sort of fella who lived on his wits, a survivor who would never go hungry. Terry, on the other hand, was more entrepreneurial, with a couple of successful businesses under his belt back home and always looking to expand his empire.

I also got the impression that Terry could survive in Jamie's world. He appeared more than capable of getting his hands dirty if need be. They were not exactly two peas from a pod but you just knew.

At this point, the park was just mental so we all decided to go sit on the wall at the edge of this big wave of people, all swathed in red, swaying and singing in every direction. It was becoming crazier and louder by the minute, 'Allez, allez, allez,' 'We've been to Hoffenheim and Maribor,' 'Poor Scouser Tommy,' and many other songs. They had been reverberating around Anfield and beyond all season and were now being belted out with force in the park. A great time was being had by all. Even the local plod and the Ukrainian army, of which there were plenty, seemed a little relaxed.

Don't get me wrong, any liberty taken and you would probably never see your ma again; you could end up in Siberia cracking salt for the rest of your natural. There was a serious air of menace around with these foot soldiers; a smiling threat if there is such a thing – laughing assassins.

There were almost as many of them in town as Redmen, or so it appeared. They all seemed to be in a semi-state of readiness. Relax until it happens rather than a stand ready for action attitude. Nice one comrades, fair play. This didn't go unnoticed and was greatly appreciated by the travelling hordes. The local authorities had invested heavily in these small armies.

Asking any of them for directions was nigh-on impossible, though, as it appeared most had been drafted in from other towns and cities across the country and didn't seem to know where they were either. But the mood was good and everybody seemed to be embracing the moment.

20

The Park Paraffin

THE PARK was alive and kicking, and locals were even trying their luck. Dynamo Kyiv fans were brazenly wandering into the park proudly showing their colours and waving their flags, but this was never going to be a problem. There were cameras and phones clicking away as this was one big football love-in.

I sat on the park wall taking in the atmosphere, looking out for faces. Further along the wall, I recognised someone I knew from back home. He saw me and walked over to say hello. This bloke, who is not a Scouser, in fact he's not even English, had been travelling to watch the Reds for many years. Every game you attended you would always see him on your travels.

Tage Hersted is in fact Norwegian. I mentioned that the odd tourist does blend in and become part of it all. Well, he's local now and has been living in the city with his family for many years. It made sense as he used to travel to all of the games from Norway. He eventually realised it would be cheaper and easier just to move to Liverpool.

Tage probably wasn't the pioneer but he is now a major player in bringing fans from overseas to Anfield. He is now living the dream as he is part owner of a hotel that recently opened, which is only 300 yards from Anfield. Hotel TIA (This is Anfield) is everything LFC. It's like a mini museum with a few beds and bars thrown in. You never know who you may bump into there too, as Tage is also personal friends with many of the Liverpool legends who often frequent his place.

While sat chatting with Jamie and Tage, I noticed a scruffy old boy who was alone on a bench near to the park's main entrance. He was just sat there, taking things in. I studied this situation with interest while still trying to enjoy every second of what was going on all around me. I kept glancing back over to the main entrance of the park, in the direction of what had caught my eye in the first place. This unkempt old man remained sat on his bench, mesmerised by what was unfolding all around him.

He had a striking resemblance to Grandad from *Only Fools and Horses*. He'd probably never experienced anything of this magnitude before, especially in this very public park that he classed as home. His garden was packed to bursting having been taken over by tens of thousands of Scousers along with a few of the locals and tourists who had mingled in, all invading his space, his home.

That afternoon, I witnessed something in the park that will stay with me forever. What was about to unfold in front of me was one of the most heartwarming yet heartbreaking scenes I have ever observed. There were a couple of ladies all decked in red stood close by to him. I smiled to myself as he stood up and insisted the ladies have his seat. I found it amazing that a man in his position still felt it right to be chivalrous.

After giving up his perch, he then lay on the grass with a big smile on his face. What struck me was that it was a sincere, genuine smile. He honestly gave me the impression that he was really enjoying what was going on all around him. Almost as if he was acting like the perfect host, welcoming all to his manor.

At first people were mainly ignoring him and leaving him be but as the park started to swell with numbers, his smile was to become a whole lot wider. I observed him closely as the afternoon progressed into the early evening. Kick-off was approaching and as fans were starting to make their way out of the park towards the stadium, he was approached by a couple of Redmen. After a little conversation there were handshakes all round, pats on his back and as the lads bid their farewells, they left him with a small picnic of booze. Moments later, more and more Reds fans were going over to him, almost in queue form. They too were slapping him on the back, shaking his hand and stuffing cash into his hands, pockets and anywhere else he could store it. This money was almost like Monopoly money to us and not in a Billy Big Bollocks way, just in the fact that we were having great difficulty in trying to spend it, as everything was so cheap.

Undoubtedly this old boy had never seen such riches, let alone held it in the palms of his hands. He had his pockets full of the stuff. The Redmen were giving him beer by the crateful. Then half a bottle of Scotch found its way into his possession, closely followed by many other bottles of spirits. At the same time, bundles of cash were handed to him. He was like a pig in gold-laced shit, encrusted with diamonds and topped off with truffles.

Once he realised what was happening, he went into some kind of ritual, praying with thanks to the skies and then kissing the ground beneath his feet. It must have been like a lottery win for him; he probably had enough cash stuffed into his pockets to go on a couple of football trips himself!

When we finally made our move and left the park, I noticed the old boy was fast asleep on the grass, surrounded by what can only be described as a pop-up booze bank. He had been gifted enough stock to feed all of his unfortunate community wherever they may have been in this city.

'We've just killed him,' was one of the last comments I heard as we exited the park. Then reality hit me straight between the eyes with a big smack of conscience. All I could think was, 'Will this old-timer live to spend it, would he die a happy man?'

I really must start listening to Donna and stop over-thinking things.

What a sobering thought that comment was. Bless you old boy, life must have been pretty shit for you.

I sincerely hoped he would recover but I seriously doubted he would.

21

This Is What We Came For

I DECIDED to answer the call of nature one last time before leaving the park and heading off towards the ground, although the park's facilities were a little short in number to say the least. The lengthy queues to gain entry to the portaloos were enough themselves to make your eyes water, although while waiting I spotted a face from many years ago. Bucko was old school, who had been there, seen it and done it all before, and was still bobbing around Europe, trying to stay out of trouble. As I keep saying, a nod, a wink or a handshake is all it takes. It's like you've never been away.

The toilets themselves were something that you wouldn't really enter, unless you were so desperate that you couldn't function properly because of the pain. These closets must have made the ones they have at Glastonbury seem quite hygienic. With the amount of drinking that had gone on that afternoon, I suppose it was inevitable that these little cabins were going to take a hammering.

The only alternative, well for a bloke anyway, was the tried and trusted method of finding a big tree with not too many people around. The problem was that with so many of the local and national army knocking about, this option was never really on the table, unless you fancied a whack on the back of your head and getting dragged off to who knows where and for how long. Wait in line and pray you don't piss yourself was the most sensible route to take.

On the short trip from the park back down towards the stadium you could hear, feel and see the excitement growing even more. The atmosphere was incredible; thousands upon thousands of Redmen were swarming towards the ground. It was a human tsunami surging towards the Olimpiyskiy, all singing and dancing. This is what we're here for. Still missing Donna though.

Our friends from Spain, the Real Madrid fans, were utterly and completely outnumbered; surely they couldn't help but feel intimidated, although not in a threatened kind of way by any stretch of the imagination. Everyone was in high spirits. There are countless photographs and videos on social media of the Redmen and Real Madrid fans partying together. I can honestly say that there wasn't one incident I witnessed that could be construed as anything else but a happy party. 'This is what the old derby days used to be like,' I thought to myself.

The atmosphere continued all the way down to the stadium. Walking back down the high street, I thought I caught sight of somebody moving rather sharply behind my left shoulder, trying to come in on my blind side. From experience you get a sense in these situations so with my radar on, I waited for this fella to get closer and make his move. As he drew closer, I swung around to front him. It was a bloke from work who was attempting to steal one in on me from behind, only as a wind-up of course, or at least I hoped it was! I quickly realised that Jamie was on his tail, as he was on mine. This could have easily ended in tears as Jamie was a split second away from sticking this fella on his arse. The Kyiv police force and their army buddies were only yards away and may well have shown a little more interest in this little playful incident than was warranted.

Once outside the stadium, Jamie was roaming everywhere, off talking to little troops of boys, small teams from all over Liverpool. You could certainly tell these lads were serious players. These were naughty boys, the type you don't ever want to f**k with. Jamie had connections everywhere. How do you tell if a man doesn't give a shit? Just watch him roll a joint while the Ukrainian army are feet away and armed to the teeth. That takes some balls if you ask me. Maybe these fellas just weren't worried about the consequences. Brave or stupid? You decide.

It was time to make our way into the ground and as we queued alongside the thousands of other fans waiting to enjoy the final showdown of our season, more and more faces were appearing as we edged closer to the first checkpoint. It really was a blur of nods, shouts, waves and thumbs-up gestures everywhere you looked. Everyone had come out to play at a sort of unorganised reunion. You were going to be there and hoped others could make it too. At most normal reunions the eventual turnout is quite often higher than expected, and this was no exception.

Although the amount of fans gathering outside was already high and growing by the minute, the situation never got anywhere near to an overcrowding issue. The Robocop authorities manning the barriers were well on top and their lines were in orderly fashion.

Once beyond the exterior barriers there was an expanse of ground before you reached the turnstiles themselves. As we edged closer to our entrance point, what really surprised me was the amount of double clicking that was going on. This was one of the reasons that access was beginning to slow down the nearer we got to the turnstiles. This was where the unfortunate part-time young stewards were working and they were the ones who had to put up with the frontline shit, as usual. I have witnessed similar scenes on countless occasions. I felt sympathy for these boys and girls. Double clicking was happening at every turnstile; some got caught, some got in. The ones caught were just pushed back into the crowds and set free to try again.

One thing I have never understood is when catching somebody trying to bunk into a stadium, why do the authorities always eject them the same way they attempted to get in? Surely it would be a lot easier and quicker, not to mention safer and a lot less crowd-provoking, if the culprit was allowed entry through the turnstile with the natural flow of people. Once inside the stadium, they could then be dealt with. I have witnessed this happening on countless occasions at stadiums all across Europe, as well as at home. I wouldn't dare to estimate the number of fans who succeeded in getting in without a ticket this time.

At Wembley back in 1978, I myself had employed this tactic to gain entry to our European Cup Final against Club Brugge from Belgium. In fact, I double clicked on six occasions that night, getting thrown out on five of them by the same Cockney steward until eventually he said to me, 'F**k me Scouse, I'm pissed off throwing you out, you deserve to get in, go on f**k off before I change my mind.'

I was 17 back then and so full of energy. He was never going to keep me out. He would have had to spend the entire match chasing me round the old Twin Towers. I'd worn him down and I think he knew it too as he threw in the towel. 'Cheers mate,' I shouted back with a huge smile on my face as I ran off, up towards the terracing.

I could hardly believe my eyes that this tactic was still being so commonly used and executed with so much success 40 years on. From what I had seen, the number attempting this method in Kyiv was at least on par with that night at Wembley. It was supposed to be so much easier to bunk in anywhere back in the 1970s than in the modern era, or so we are led to believe. Not on this evidence! As well as this night in Kyiv, our previous Champions League Final in Athens had also presented very similar opportunities for ticketless fans. There weren't even any turnstiles in Athens, just big gates believe it or not. Are lessons never learned? Alas, usually when it's too late.

Once inside the turnstiles at the Olimpiyskiy there was a huge outdoor area, with a concourse selling the usual food and drinks. Plus there was the usual array of UEFA merchandise to be had, at vastly inflated prices of course. Thirty pounds for a baseball cap; a tenner for a programme. Do these people have no shame?

Jamie was after a baseball cap for one of his presents but the tourists were filling the queues to the max. He wasn't having any of that so he decided to bunk into the line near the front. The muscles stewarding this event around the kiosks were fully briefed on the collecting habits of Scousers. Jamie was attempting to order some merchandise and just turn and walk. A decent enough ploy but for the fact that these burly stewards were on top of their game. Jamie was sussed and decided to abandon his plan before it got started, which I thought was rather wise.

No one in their right mind would risk losing a Champions League Final seat for a baseball cap, surely! Sometimes you just have to wipe your mouth and walk away. Jamie later left his seat at half-time and indeed came back wearing a baseball cap. I never did ask how he obtained it.

All through this season's campaign I'd felt extremely confident as to our ultimate destination, and there were so many tenuous links flying around the city that you couldn't help but feel confident. Royal weddings, new Dr Who, the Pope dying, all of our previous victories were against teams in white – however tenuous it was didn't really matter, it was a link and we were having it.

We'd had such a memorable season so far and the first half an hour of this game would give us much optimism that it would continue. There was so much belief among our fans that this would be our crowning glory. Few could argue that this Liverpool team would not have been worthy winners. After such an exciting season that we had all witnessed, who wouldn't believe? 'Me and my bird are trying for our sixth' as one flag proclaimed.

The scene inside the stadium was the usual three-quarters red and a quarter for the opposition. As is the norm at away games, the fans will more or less stand wherever they want;

it's seen as an opportunity to stand or even sit next to friends and family, exactly as it used to be and should still be today, some would argue.

The atmosphere was booming, mainly because of a new song that had found its way into the Kop's repertoire, 'Allez, allez, allez.' Probably not since the days of the Fernando Torres song had I heard our fans totally unite and sing with such passion, not to mention the bouncing that accompanies it.

After having a good mooch around the stand trying to find the best vantage point, Jamie and I settled on a good perch and within minutes we were joined by the Carney brothers. It is so difficult to describe but when you are there, in among your own people, all experiencing the same thing collectively, then the feeling can become quite overwhelming for some.

As the teams appeared with the Champions League theme belting out, the hairs were up on the back of my neck. UEFA's anthem was quickly drowned out by the deafening noise emanating from the travelling Kop, cascading down across the stands. Believe me when I say that there truly is no other place on earth to be. At that precise moment life doesn't get any better. Absolutely nothing compares or even comes close, apart from family matters.

The game started quite well for the Reds and in no way did we get the impression that we were there just to make up the numbers. We were there on merit; nobody could argue against that. We were there and the boys were doing a decent job too.

The lads were more than holding their own, until that t**t Sergio Ramos had a say in proceedings after 30 minutes or so. Would you want someone like him in your team? My own view is that he's not for me. Or maybe he is! The debate could rage on for an eternity. Do you think he would have got away with what he did if Steven Gerrard or Jamie Carragher were still around? I think not. I remember a game at Anfield where all three were on the pitch: Liverpool 4 Real Madrid 0. Señor Ramos was as quiet as a mouse that night. I'm not saying that we would have won 4-0 again, or even won, but maybe Mo Salah would have seen the game out and possibly had an influence along the way. But this final will go down in history as a Real Madrid victory so credit where it's due.

There was, and always will be as far as the fans are concerned though, a huge sense of injustice at not being able to compete on a level playing field. We often hear that there is more than one way to win a football game these days. Job done, Sergio!

That being said, the Liverpool fans showed an enormous amount of dignity and class, not to mention support. Most stayed beyond the final whistle to applaud the boys after the game. How many fans of other teams do that? Most these days get off on the final whistle, some even long before then, if things aren't going their way.

I mentioned earlier in this book that Jamie's character is a good sort; he has morals and values in all the right places. At the final whistle he was scanning the crowd, just looking around, possibly gauging people's reactions. Maybe he was just looking for anyone he recognised. All of a sudden and without warning, he was off. Without saying a word to any of us as he moved up towards the back of the stand, climbing over rows and rows of seats and squeezing past people as he went, climbing higher and higher. I kept a close eye on him just in case someone or something had upset him. He reached his destination where in among the red hordes was some young kid. This lad was probably around 13 or 14 years old and was sobbing away after witnessing his beloved Liverpool being cheated out of the result. Jamie embraced this kid, gave him a big hug and offered some words of comfort.

How can a fella who is such a top-drawer scally, so out for what he can get that you can almost see the Artful Dodger living and breathing inside of him, be so compassionate? How can someone who is this kind of character be so caring, especially to a complete stranger?

If you didn't know Jamie, you could easily make the mistake of thinking this boy has no morals. He looks and sometimes behaves like a proper wrong 'un but he has all of the above, and tons of it too. Maybe he reserves this side of himself for his kindred spirits.

After our team had completed their lap of honour it was time for the red hordes to vacate the stadium and start drifting away into the night. People were a little subdued; who wouldn't be? This wasn't the end of the road though, far from it. I think everyone would agree that the mood leaving the stadium was one of oh well, what another great adventure this season has been.

Danke Herr Klopp, and if we ever get our hands on that gobshite Ramos!

The walk back up through town and past Shevvy Park only took about 20 minutes. All along the way, the thousands of Redmen were surprisingly still quite jovial. They were wandering off in different directions and into different bars and restaurants to carry on regardless. The hundreds of armed forces lined along the route were also in a relaxed mood. Respect again, comrades.

We all managed to get back to our taxis at around 1am on the Sunday, and it was a stick or twist kind of dilemma. Should we stay and have a beer in a local hostelry or should we make a move? The boys were quite dry after being in an alcohol-free zone for the last few hours but the drivers were itching to get started, so sensibly we decided to get off for their wellbeing.

22

D'akuju Kyiv

IT HAD taken us around 66 hours to get to Kyiv. Three Amp was determined it wasn't going to take that long to get home. 'Every man for himself,' he announced! 'Bollocks to the convoy, we're going for it.' He hated those elongated pit stops; however, Jamie still had a little shopping to do on the way home, so stops weren't completely off the agenda.

Earlier, when we had assembled back at the taxis, I asked the drivers if they had managed to find a ticket and get to see the game. It turned out that since most of them were Blues they didn't even try looking. They were happy enough to find a restaurant, sit down, have a nice meal and watch it on TV.

Donna will tell you that I am not the best eater in the world. I eat on the move and eat badly most of the time. After three days of eating on our feet, even I was desperate for a knife and fork in my hands. It's funny how we miss the simplest things in life.

I asked the boys how the game had looked on TV as it can often appear very different from the one that you have just witnessed live. Most were in agreement that the Reds were hard done by but put up a decent fight. At the end of the conversation, it came to light that Everton-tattooed Terry, the owner, was the only one who was jumping around fist-pumping as Liverpool's demise unfolded!

Earlier I had mentioned to the boys that although he was a Blue, he was our Blue and I hoped that no one took exception to his new tat. We needed to look out for him, least of all because he was one of the drivers. Confrontation was a distinct possibility and can sometimes happen if someone has had too many beers. You may just be unlucky enough to run into someone who simply wants to tell you what he thinks of his neighbours.

It doesn't matter who you support but if you're walking around with a tattoo displaying an emblem of a rival team then you need to be smart; cover it up for a start. I'm not sure I would have felt so protective if I had witnessed his fist-pumping actions and celebrations at the restaurant though. My two brothers are both bitter Blue boys, so I shouldn't have been too surprised really. Three Amp and the rest of them were a little more sympathetic and their attitude was that they wanted us to win, although not for the glory of the club, they would never condone or encourage that. They wanted the Reds to win for us boys and girls who had crossed Europe in numbers and by any means possible. Fair play to them.

We finally left the beautiful and accommodating city of Kyiv and its welcoming inhabitants at around 1.30am. Most people dressed in red had found it extremely difficult to spend their cash and as we pulled away people still had pockets full of this Monopoly money.

We set off on the main road out of town and only about an hour or so away from Kyiv we hit a service station to refuel. Up until this point the convoy had managed to stay together. Three Amp really was serious about going it alone from there and putting his foot down, so much so that he offered to pay for any fuel we needed and would claim it back from Terry when he got home. Terry was carrying the fuel card for all of the taxis so if we were to make a run for it, we would need to fund the trip ourselves initially.

The troops were off the taxis and into the shop and cafe across the forecourt. I was one of the first off and went into the deli part of the shop, enquiring if there was any food on offer. 'Closed,' came the stern reply from a grumpy old lady behind the counter. This not-too-friendly old dear must have thought I was on my own, so she couldn't be arsed and chased me. It was 2.30am so I understood her logic. No more than three minutes after she had turned me away, I turned to look behind me and there she was, stood with a huge smile on her face, counter open, grills restarted and setting up to do a roaring trade. Everyone was off the taxis and had tumbled in to her little deli. All were hell bent on disposing of their Monopoly money. People were just throwing cash at her, hand over fist. Good luck to her.

Money was lavished on cigarettes; at a pound a packet some thought they could move these on when they got home, and therefore hopefully recoup some of their outlay for the trip. Big Gary from the nutty bus was even more entrepreneurial. This clever cookie was buying power tools at a fraction of the cost back home. Maybe he had the same idea as them or possibly he was going into the tool hire business, who knows?

Taxis and people refuelled, we finally got going once more. Three Amp and Terry decided that they were going to push for the Polish border with around four hours each of straight driving. The next three hours or so flew by, probably due to the fact that all the passengers in our taxi were sound asleep.

The next stop was good timing for breakfast and our taxi emptied into another service station. After we opened the tailgate to let Jamie out, he awoke and asked our location. 'Still in the Ukraine, mate,' Terry said to him. He got out of his bed, had a little stretch and lit a ciggie. 'For f**k's sake Jamie, we're parked in the middle of a petrol forecourt here!' shouted Terry. 'Shit, sorry boys, didn't realise,' came the reply. He had actually lit up a smoke before he had even opened his eyes!

After his little bollocking, Jamie pulled himself together and wandered off in the direction of the shop to stretch his legs. Can anyone explain to me how someone who is wearing only a t-shirt, football shorts with no pockets and only socks on their feet, wanders off into a shop and then comes back with food in one hand, drinks in the other and one of those foot-long toy wagons stuffed under his arm? Just where does someone hide something of that size? Another gift was taken care of, as well as getting fed and watered.

23

Walking The Cow

ALL BACK on the taxis and we were off once again, steaming ahead for the border crossing.

The plan was to hit the border, hopefully get through without any problems, then head back to Wrocław for a one-night stay. We all needed to rest up properly, especially the drivers. These boys were displaying tremendous willpower and discipline that came from being regimented.

I completely understand now what my dad used to bang on about, how national service should be reintroduced for all the young tearaways these days. By that I mean the tearaways from when I was in my youth. It's possibly a tad hypocritical I'd say, given the fact that Pop was a fully fledged Teddy Boy back in his young adulthood. Correct me if I'm wrong but weren't they the first generation of youths to rebel? I can see what he was trying to say though, sign up the wrong 'uns and teach them some discipline and respect.

About an hour away from the Polish border a quick stop literally in the middle of nowhere was required to answer nature's call. I always find it amusing when normally it is only one person who is bursting and needs to pull over somewhere, otherwise they will piss themselves, yet when the bus does eventually stop, the entire travelling party takes advantage. We pulled over in to what we thought was a deserted wooded area with nothing around but fields and trees, or so we assumed. The boys were off the taxi again and pissing like racehorses once more.

Bollocks, where did *he* come from? Stood alongside our taxi was one of the Ukrainian plod. 'This could get shitty,' I thought to myself, as I was attempting to make myself presentable as quickly as I could without being noticed. Everyone else was back in the taxi, sat there smiling. 'Thank you very much, have a nice day,' was all the officer said after having a quick look at the paperwork belonging to our drivers. Wow, what a completely different attitude to the one we had encountered on the way in. If the toilet break had happened around 48 hours earlier, I'm almost certain that would have been as far as we would have got. The consequences could have been quite severe. We could well have been done for indecent exposure!

I've mentioned more than once the fact that Three Amp likes to be organised. 'Jamie, you best get out of your bed and climb up front with the rest of us now, before we hit the border,' he commanded, although we were still at least an hour away. Ten minutes later, Jamie still hadn't responded to the request, so Three Amp pleaded, 'Jay, come up front mate so the plod don't get the hump.' Three Amp had a point; Jamie was travelling in the boot after all.

After a further request another ten minutes later, Jamie started to stir. His method of re-joining the land of the living was to basically climb over everybody. People were getting hit with his knees, elbows and feet as he was moaning and groaning along the way about having to leave his bed. It was just then that I saw one of the most unusual sights ever – it was so bizarre it couldn't have been real. Maybe I was over-tired or maybe my mind was playing tricks on me. Tentatively I asked, 'Did anyone else just see that?' 'I did but I wasn't sure, it didn't seem to register, I'm still trying to process what I've just seen,' said Terry.

Others stared but didn't say a word. We had been travelling for miles and miles without seeing anything but fields and the odd farm animal in the distance, when literally in the middle of nowhere, we noticed an old lady stood by the side of the road, talking to a cow! She wasn't only talking to it, she appeared to be giving it a right bollocking. She had it on a lead as she was wagging her finger in the direction of the beast. Even funnier was the fact that the cow was hanging its head in shame as her finger was pointing rapidly in its direction. 'You can just picture the scene at home an hour ago,' I said. 'Tityana, that f*****g cow's out!' 'Have you left that bleeding gate open again?' 'Well, I've been asking you to mend that gate for weeks, it's no surprise he keeps f*****g off,' quipped Jamie in his best female Ukrainian accent. We were all in fits of laughter imagining the possible scenario that could have led to this situation. She looked as if she was giving the cow a right earful for getting on his toes again.

Pure gold, it certainly lifted everyone's spirits. Three Amp almost had to stop driving as he couldn't see straight through the tears of laughter streaming down his face.

The taxi had recomposed itself by the time we reached the border crossings, and we seriously needed to. There we were again, stuck in huge delays with rows and rows of Ukrainian soldiers, armed to the teeth as before with AK47s, hand guns, the lot. I can understand their nervous disposition but surely even Putin wouldn't come in through their front door. These boys and girls were a lot more compassionate on the way out though, very much like their police force. They were probably glad to see the back of 40,000 Liverpool fans and there were a lot more smiles delivered with the questions they asked on our way out.

We were held up at the border for what seemed like an age and as the weather was still glorious, I decided to stretch my legs, pay a visit to the little boys' room and generally have a nose around. Granted, there wasn't a lot to look at apart from wagons, cars and coaches as far as the eye could see. If you wanted a burst at these toilets then that wasn't a problem, but the problems arose if you needed anything else. There was no toilet paper on the inside of these filthy conveniences. If you wanted a number two then you had to purchase the paper from an old woman who was sat outside the toilets. The toilet paper she was selling was that shiny old stuff you used to get at school, or at least you did back in my day anyway. Once again, our servicemen and their wet wipes proved invaluable.

After leaving the toilet I started to have a slow stroll back towards our taxi. I almost bumped into a Ukrainian soldier who was absolutely colossal, so huge that I did well to avoid contact. I turned a corner and there he was, stood in front of me looking all Rambo-like but without the bandana and string vest. He was dressed in grey instead of green with all the matching accessories such as an AK47, hand grenade, a truncheon, handcuffs, the full works. This fella was a walking arsenal and he spoke like Arnold Schwarzenegger. If I hadn't already been to the toilet then I'm certain this killing machine would have helped me out without even trying. He looked so menacing.

We have often heard it said that 'looks can deceive' and it turned out that this Ramboski was a really cool bloke. We both stopped and looked at each other, only for a few seconds but it seemed a lot longer, then he just smiled and asked me if I was okay. 'Only stretching my legs,' I said to him as he reached into his shirt pocket for a packet of cigarettes. My new mate then removed his AK from over his shoulder, sat down and asked me to join him.

We sat on a grass verge at the side of the building, his sub-machine gun beside him as he lit a cigarette. We had a laugh together and he was a very decent bloke. He just wanted to chat football, have a ciggie and a giggle. Although he was a Dynamo Kyiv supporter, he told me that his favourite player of all time was El Niño, Fernando Torres, Liverpool's number nine. Who could ever forget that first couple of seasons at Anfield for Nando? I understood his adoration.

As we chatted away the official Liverpool team coach crawled up towards the border checkpoint. My mate Ramboski was up on his feet in a flash, acting all official once again, looking all threatening, just as he was meant to. This was my cue to leave, so I said my farewells with a hug and a handshake. I desperately wanted a photo shaking his hand but protocol said no to that.

There was more than a little activity around the big red bus for obvious reasons. The border crossing was very busy to say the least, with most of the vehicles carrying Liverpool supporters back home.

'Relax, boys,' I said as I got back to our taxi. 'There is no way anyone from the club will be on board that. That thing will be full of corporates.'

Jamie was showing a little more interest than most in the bus and wandered off for a closer investigation. The door was open given that the weather was glorious once again. The bus was hardly moving so I doubt there was a health and safety issue there. Like the rest of us, their driver was waiting for a signal to move forward and his second man was sitting closest to the open door. Jamie idled up and while still stood on the pavement tried to have a little look inside. With a smile on his face he jokingly asked, 'Any room for a little one on there mate?' 'There's enough little ones on here already pal,' said the driver with a smile on his face too. 'Well, any room for a big one then?' Jamie said, grinning at his own question. 'Yeah, you are a big one, aren't you?' was the retort from the driver's second man, who wasn't half as smiley as his colleague. 'You cheeky c**t, I'll pull you from that bus by your f****g Adam's apple,' Jamie threatened as his mood quickly changed.

He made a move to board the bus but the driver very cleverly and quickly hit the close door button. It was a job well done because Jamie would have carried out his threat, no question.

Why are some people so up their own arses? They get a decent job and they think they are the dog's bollocks. The main driver seemed sound, so why was his second man behaving like an idiot? Enjoy what you've got mate, no need for the Billy Big Bollocks shite, who are you trying to impress?

The driver had acted quickly and prevented the situation from escalating. For no reason whatsoever, this was another situation that could have easily turned very nasty indeed.

There was absolutely no need for this comment and maybe it wouldn't have provoked most people, but Jamie is made of different things and took it more to heart. If things had kicked off, you can bet your last pound it wouldn't have been the drivers of the Liverpool bus who got the headlines, it would have been 'them Scousers again'. Think about that next time mate, a smile goes a long way.

After all, we are the people who pay the dollars, contribute to your wages, and put ourselves in all kinds of situations to follow the boys around Europe and beyond. Unlike you and your colleagues, we do it with no safety net around us whatsoever. You get looked after on your foreign trips, you get well fed, along with classy accommodation thrown in, you also get paid to do it and yet people like you are probably the least deserving.

We were drawn away from this scenario due to the shouts from our taxi that told us that we were moving at last, and we were finally waving goodbye to the beautiful and extremely hospitable Ukraine.

24

Return To Wrocław
(Where the f**k is Jamie?)

OUR TAXI was finally on its way, back into Poland. The plan was to get back to Wrocław for the night, then the Carney brothers and the Bristol beauts were leaving us the next morning and flying home. That was going to make the remainder of the trip home even better for Jamie and I as we had an eight-seater taxi with two drivers and two passengers, all to ourselves – pure luxury.

As we meandered along the motorway, we encountered some roadworks which meant a little detour, although it was not a problem as the servicemen had the GPS on their phones up and running. We were winding our way through little villages and towns, admiring the tranquillity and natural beauty of such places, when we came across one that had a real busy vibe going on. We couldn't help notice an extraordinary number of cars parked up for such a small place. Most of the cars were double parked along the little side roads, making it difficult for us to manoeuvre along at any sort of pace.

The whole village was very picturesque and as we turned a corner there it was, the only reason this little place could have been so busy.

It was a vision of natural beauty; an oasis in the middle of nowhere. It was now pretty obvious why this little village had an abundance of cars and was full of visitors – scantily clad beauties and Adonises, ice cream vans, barbecues, the lot. This local attraction was basically a lake surrounded by beautiful scenery. Everywhere you looked, people were jumping off rocks of varying heights into the shimmering water below. They were swimming, lazing around on lilos and pedalos, generally having fun and lots of it. The weather was still amazing and of course the locals were out in their hundreds, making the most of their Sunday afternoon off. Local boys and girls were launching themselves off huge rocks into this vision of paradise. 'F*****g loons,' someone commented.

This natural beauty spot was given the name of Suicide Creek by Karl. I suggested that we should stop and experience this little piece of heaven if only for an hour or so. 'It's not every day that you get the chance to do something like this,' I said, 'especially on a football trip!'

The general consensus was that most were in favour, but the Bristol beauts were very non-committal to say the least. They hinted that they needed to get to their hotel to check out before 8pm. So what? If you're late then just pay the extra for the hotel. The request to stop as mainly ignored though and the further away we slipped from this little gem the more it truly did appear to be nothing more than an oasis. There one minute, gone the next. 'You missed an opportunity there boys,' I said ruefully.

The Bristolians were a little more unpopular than at any time before. Don't get me wrong, they weren't bad lads, but were probably just not up to speed with the locals from back home. Good old Scousers are up for most things given half a chance. I got the impression that the occupants of our little taxi were flagging anyway. There wasn't that much of a fight put up to stop in the first place. I'd say the Bristol lads won by a technical knockout.

We re-joined the motorway and a while later decided on one more stop before the final push into Wrocław. Off the taxi we all clambered and before we could even stretch our legs, they were on us – Romanian travellers trying to sell us sets of kitchen knives. They looked very impressive as they displayed their fencing skills and demonstrated just how sharp their knives actually were. Holding up pieces of paper and slicing through them with ease, these Romanian versions of Zorro were all over the place.

'How much?' asked Jamie as one of them approached us. 'Forty Euros,' came the reply. 'F**k off, not paying that,' Jamie responded. The next offer was €30. 'No chance mate,' Jamie continued. 'Okay, give me €20!' I watched with interest as the bartering continued, knowing full well who the winner of this little contest was going to be. 'Not interested bud,' said Jamie, standing his ground. 'Come on, give me €20,' pleaded Zorro. 'Take em off your hands for five lad!' 'No no, €20, I need €20!' 'Five or we don't want them,' was Jamie's last offer. 'Okay, give me five,' said Zorro, beaten at his own game.

'Give us three sets then will yer lad!' Jamie said after getting a thumbs-up from myself and Paul, indicating that we would have a set each too. Jamie had the deal done and the blades were put in to the back of our taxi. The Romanian entrepreneur must have walked away thinking to himself, 'What the f**k just happened there?'

Off we went into yet another Subway, in part of the service station. Once again, I would have killed for a proper sit-down meal with a knife and fork. I had just bought some knives so I suppose I only needed a fork and a nice meal to complete the set.

Jamie had broken his sunglasses earlier in the trip so was on the lookout for some new ones. He walked straight into the shop alongside the cafe, looking for any sunglasses that may have been on display. He found the stand and slowly turned it around looking for a pair that he liked the look of. Decision made, he picked them up and placed them on top of his head.

He then got himself in the queue waiting to order his meal. Once his hot sandwich arrived, he made his way to the till. The young girl behind the counter then proceeded to tell him how much he owed for his lunch. Jamie suddenly went off on one, complaining that his sandwich was cold and not the one he ordered. He grumbled a little more but paid his dues then walked out of the shop, along with his newly acquired sunglasses still on top of his head. A classic distraction technique?

Whenever we had a pit stop, and there were plenty of them, we would all pile back on the taxi in the way most people do, through the doors. Jamie, though, would lift up the tailgate and climb back into his bedroom. He would then normally get his head down and try to sleep until the next stop; usually you wouldn't get a peep out of him.

Around ten minutes after leaving this last service station there was a shout of, 'Jamie, is there any water back there?'

No reply was forthcoming from the back of the taxi. 'Jay, you got any water back there mate?' Three Amp, who was having a break from driving, turned around and looked into Jamie's bedroom. 'Shit, Steve, Jamie's not here,' he said alarmingly. 'Yeah sure,' I replied casually, thinking it was a wind-up. 'Steve, I am not f****n' messin', he's not f****n' 'ere!' His tone was becoming more anxious. 'Have a look under the bags, he'll be asleep somewhere in there,' I continued calmly, still believing it was a joke. 'Ste, I'm telling you mate, you're not listening, he's not f****n' 'ere.' Three Amp was now shouting at me. Finally realising he must be serious, I looked into Jamie's bedroom myself. Shit, he was serious, Jamie wasn't there!

I immediately pulled my phone out to call him. 'Jamie, where the f**k are you lad?' I asked, relieved that he'd at least answered his phone and had not encountered any problems with the Romanians and their knives. 'I'm sunbathing on a picnic bench at the service station. I came out the toilets and you had all f****d off,' he replied with a relaxed tone. 'Don't move, we're on our way back,' I told him. 'Don't rush, it's nice here. I'm just chillin', see yer in a bit,' he said, as calm as you like, oblivious to the panic he had just caused.

'Who saw him last?' I asked. Karl said the last time he'd seen Jamie, he was trying to re-sell the kitchen knives back to some other gypsies, for a profit of course. Terry had his GPS switched on, trying to find a route back to pick him up. 'Bollocks!' he exclaimed. 'It's about a 20-mile round trip.'

Up until this point, half of the convoy had somehow managed to stay together. We made contact with the lead taxi and Terry sensibly suggested it was pointless everybody turning around so they proceeded with their journey towards Wrocław. We were on our own! After continuing west for what seemed like an eternity, we finally reached the first exit junction. We came off on a slip road that enabled us to turn around and head back east to pick Jamie up. It was a good 20 minutes or so later when we drove past the service station where Jamie was stranded.

There were no access roads to reach him as we were on the opposite carriageway. Frustratingly, we had to continue driving and find another exit so we could perform a U-turn once more. This would eventually put us on the same carriageway that Jamie was on, awaiting our return, sunbathing. It's a tough life.

Terry left the motorway on the next slip road to make the final U-turn. We came across a police checkpoint, which we thought was a bit strange as we were in the middle of nowhere. We pulled up behind a line of cars and lorries who all seemed to be attracting the attention of a local policeman. The officer was stood next to his motorbike parked up at the side of the road. He was stopping and breathalysing the drivers of every vehicle that came his way. One after one, this plod was simply shoving his breathalyser into the mouth of every driver. No antibacterial wipes here, straight from one gob into another. Random and possibly a good idea on the face of it. But I ask you, is there not a health and hygiene issue here? Who knows what the other people being tested had got up to earlier that day, or even the night before?

I quite enjoy driving, but at this exact moment I was more than happy to be a passenger. I don't think my stomach would have stood up to this kind of oral examination. It wasn't very nice for Terry, who in his state of shock, forgot to use his own wet wipes. With the ordeal soon over, he sailed through clean as a whistle. I wouldn't have expected anything less from this pro.

After abandoning Jamie earlier we eventually pulled back into the services where we had left him. Jamie was doing exactly what he told us he was doing, sunbathing on a picnic table. He was also in possession of another present to add to his collection.

'What would you have done if we hadn't come back, Jay?' he was asked. 'Just piggybacked on to the next load of Scousers passing through,' he replied. 'Not a problem!' Jamie clearly hadn't given any thought to any passport issues that may have occurred further down the line. His was still in his bag in our taxi.

That's a pretty cool reaction if you ask me. I would have shit myself for sure but not much worries this character. Once he had loaded his booty into the taxi and checked back into his bedroom, we were off again, Wrocław-bound.

25

Indecent Proposal

WE REACHED the centre of Wrocław at around 9pm. The city itself is very charming and beautiful, somewhere you would have no problem at all taking your squeeze for a nice break, and the cost of living there is very reasonable. Even though it was more expensive than Kyiv, it was still a lot cheaper than back home.

After running around for a while and getting caught up in one-way systems, we eventually dropped the Bristol beauts at their hotel so they could check out. We arranged to meet them in the main square later that evening. The GPS was reset and we followed the route towards our hotel. As we ventured further out of the city centre looking out for our digs, the districts were becoming a little less appealing. A short drive later, we rolled up into a moody part of town which would be our base for the night.

Although it looked rough upon arrival, once we checked in, the hotel wasn't as bad as it had first appeared. Inside was clean, tidy and much better than our first night's stay in Wrocław.

Due to our afternoon being full of diversions, detours and dropping people off, our taxi was the last to arrive at our abode for the night. The others had arrived hours earlier, so most of the troops had already gone off and dispersed in different directions to find some entertainment and perhaps a decent meal. That was definitely my sole purpose, or at least a big priority for my night out.

Once again I was sharing with Jamie, who jumped in the shower first as soon as we had got to our room. By the time I had got cleaned up, I was last down into the bar. Jamie was sat with the boys from the nutty bus who were still enjoying a beer or two in the hotel. 'Everyone's f****d off for a pizza,' he said. 'I'm goin' into town with these boys, you comin'?' 'Course yeah,' I said, 'but I could do with a decent nosebag while we're out mate, don't really fancy pizza.' 'Yeah, we'll get one in town, I'm starvin' meself,' promised Jamie.

Three Amp was determined to get off as early as possible the following morning. He had been making noises earlier that suggested he wanted to be on the road by 6am. The plan he and Terry had for the night was to have a nice meal and a couple of beers then go back to the hotel. They were both extremely professional once again. They never bothered with town at all, they just went for a pizza in the restaurant next door to our hotel and then crashed for the night. The Carney brothers were also playing it safe as they were up at five in the morning to catch their flight back home.

So it was myself, Jamie and the nutty boys, which I thought should be interesting. Three taxis were summoned and we were soon pulling up in the town square at around 10pm.

It seemed like ages ago that we were last in Wrocław, when in fact it was only three days previous. When we arrived, the main square was a little quieter than on our last visit. On the previous Thursday night this place was rocking to the sounds of Liverpool songs but it was now Sunday. We had a quick mooch around looking for a restaurant. The usual hawkers were about trying to get us to visit their various establishments. Food was high on the agenda. 'Drink can take a back seat,' I thought to myself, especially as the drivers wanted to be on the road by six the following morning.

We were cajoled into a bar with the promise of food and were led into a big outside seating area. There was myself, Jamie, and Danny and Woodsie who had managed to break away from their main party on the nutty bus. Also in our company was a fella called John, who came from Huyton. He was off the Bible bus and I got the impression he wanted some alternative company. Danny and Woodsie looked like they could do with a break from the demands of the nutty bus too. Pints ordered and menus distributed, we were each scanning to see what was on offer as the drinks arrived. 'Sorry misters, the kitchen is now closed because we shut soon,' said the waiter.

'You said there was food,' I pleaded, more desperate than ever to sit down to a nice meal. 'Yes, I am sorry, mistake from me, everywhere close kitchens early because it is a Sunday,' he replied in his best pidgin English. Great salesman there: gets you in, gets your beer money and then pisses you off.

There's no point in complaining as you'll never win. In my experience, even if they did reopen their kitchen, think about what you could be eating. Trust me, a chef is not the kind of person you want to upset.

'Not another golden f****n' arches,' I thought. 'I can't take much more of this.'

As we scanned the town square from our seats in the beer garden, many of the lights were being switched off at the various watering holes. John suggested that we may as well have another pint while we decided what to do so we ordered another round. The drinks arrived along with more apologies from the waiter. It didn't go unnoticed though that the second round was a little more expensive than the first one. 'These f*****s are trying to have us off now,' was the general feeling among the boys. We weren't first-time day-trippers though, they thought we didn't know how it works but we've seen it a hundred times before. We could have stayed there all night and lined the owner's pockets with our Monopoly money but we weren't having any of that, so this was definitely our last drink in this establishment.

The outside seating area of the bar we were in was now deserted apart from us and one other couple who were sat in the corner. They were both probably in their early 50s and the bloke seemed a little wobbly to say the least. He got up to presumably go to the toilet and stumbled his way past us on his way inside the bar. His missus was sat on her own for a little while just taking in the surroundings of this quaint city square in the middle of Poland. After a few minutes had passed, Jamie shouted across the tables, 'You from Liverpool, girl?' The woman just smiled and replied, 'Almost – the Wirral.' 'I could just tell,' said Jamie.

Her hubby reappeared and came wobbling back to their table; he certainly seemed to be enjoying himself. He flopped down next to his wife and she told him we were returning

Redmen on our way home from Kyiv. The news sure gave this boy a shot in the arm.

It turned out that he was a Liverpool season ticket holder but was unlucky in the ballot and hadn't bagged himself a golden ticket for the final. A way of easing his pain was to take his squeeze away for a few days, which was a decent shout I thought.

To save any embarrassment on their part I will keep this couple's names private. You will understand my stance as this particular story unfolds.

Mr Wirral was chuffed to bits to be in the company of Reds in a foreign land. 'Let me get you all a drink,' he said with a slurred tongue. 'It's okay lad, there's more of us, we'll get you and your bird one,' Jamie offered.

Against our better judgement we decided to have one more there, just to be sociable with our new friends. The waiter was summoned, a round was ordered and then he come out with this ludicrous bullshit, 'The drinks are now a different price because we soon close.' 'You think we're a bunch of dickheads?' 'F****n' knobhead, you're taking the piss.' Our comments were aimed in the direction of the waiter, not in an aggressive way I must add. We are far too long in the tooth to put up with this kind of extortion so we settled our bill and we were off.

We told the Wirral couple that this bar was trying to rip us off so we were heading to the other side of the square to a boozer we were in a few nights ago. 'We'll finish up and follow you over,' said the wife.

I thought it unlikely that her hubby could walk to a taxi never mind across the town square. His second wind, although impressive, was equally short-lived. We all said our farewells and as we left the bar I shouted over, 'See you both in a bit then,' not really expecting to see either of them ever again.

We headed over and settled down in the same bar that had served us so well a few nights before. We had been in there for about 30 minutes when I told the boys that I was going to scan the square to look for that Wirral couple. I had been sat there thinking about the state Mr Wirral was in and my protective streak must have kicked in. I always feel a sense of responsibility when it comes to seeing people hammered and unable to look after themselves. It always makes me feel uneasy.

Maybe being an ex-landlord has something to do with it, or maybe it was my navy days. Whenever we were on shore leave, you always had to keep your guard up. It didn't matter what country you were in, or even what continent. I've lost count of the amount of people I have seen become unstuck because of the drink.

After only a couple of minutes walking around the square I came across them, and they were stood right in the middle not knowing too much of where they were or which way to turn. Mr Wirral was adamant that he wasn't going back to the hotel without having one last drink with the boys. He was happy to see me but I think his wife was more relieved and grateful that I had found them. She wasn't so bad but her hubby looked like he needed his bed. Although he looked and sounded worse for wear, he was still adamant that he wanted to stay out. Fair enough, who was I to tell him he needed to go back to his hotel. His wife just smiled and said to him, 'One more and that's it, we're going back to our hotel after that.'

This put a huge grin on his face and so we were off to re-join the rest of the boys.

More than a couple of rounds later and Mr Wirral was still hanging on in there. He had mentioned earlier that he was a runner and had only that morning completed either a half or full marathon before jetting away with his bride. No wonder he was struggling.

Lots of small talk took place and as often in these situations chat always gets around to other people, people you know and inevitably mutual friends. Coincidently, his wife had grown up and was friends with people I had worked with many years ago on the Wirral.

The square was quietening down and yet there still seemed to be plenty of people knocking around. The usual street beggars hadn't yet retired for the night and one suddenly landed at our feet. This one was not the usual cap out, 'spare any change guv'nor' sort of beggar, he wanted to earn his zlotys. He must have been at least 70 years of age and there he was, doing one-armed press-ups, standing on his head, all sorts of tricks most 20-year-olds couldn't manage. Credit where it's due and Jamie was straight over throwing some coin at him.

Mr Wirral was now starting to flag on a big scale and his bride was telling him they needed to be getting back to the hotel. He was still putting up some resistance to this idea but a few of the lads intervened and eventually managed to convince him that it really was time to go. A few moments later, a taxi was summoned and had pulled up to take the couple back to their hotel. As the husband was poured in by a couple of the lads, and I do mean poured, the wife took us by complete surprise. We were saying our farewells when she turned to Jamie and said completely unexpectedly, 'Jamie, I wish it was you who was taking me back to our hotel to f**k me!' I looked at Jamie in disbelief, speechless, as he had done nothing whatsoever to encourage this comment.

My feeling towards her husband as the taxi sped off into the night was 'you poor bastard'. Earlier in the evening she had made reference to the fact that although she had never been to Wrocław before, she had been to Kraków 11 times, always with her mates. The mind boggles!

Now I am no expert on marriage guidance, far from it in fact, but maybe Mr Wirral should have spent a little more time pounding his lady instead of pounding the roads doing marathons! Jamie and I just smiled to each other knowingly as we left the bar and walked off towards the taxi rank. 'Nice to get your ego massaged now and again,' I said to him.

It must have been getting into the early hours of the morning as we left the bar; the town was a little deserted by this time and food was no longer on the agenda. 'Let's just get back as we've got to be up in a couple of hours,' I said to Jamie. The only flaw with this plan was that we were on the same taxi rank as a few days ago, and it was opposite the same totty bar that I had wrestled Jamie away from on that last visit.

As we waited on the corner of the rank this big Polish woman, or should I say another female wrestler, approached us. 'Not interested,' said Jamie, before even giving her the chance to speak. 'You like girls,' she stated rather than questioned. 'No, thank you, we're getting off,' I replied. 'You want dancing girls?' she asked this time. 'No, we're good,' I reminded her. 'Come on, nice girls,' she urged persuasively.

'Don't you understand the word no?' I said, raising my voice slightly. 'Well f**k you, you two fags,' she snapped back. 'Yes, thank you, hope you have a nice evening too,' I remarked with sarcasm.

The conversation was directed more at me, or should I say I was doing most of the talking. This bruiser cast me a look as if to say 'I don't like you'. Like I gave a shit! While I was having my chat with this charming lady, Jamie had clocked the nutty boys marching past in single file down the stairs once again into this den of iniquity. He was off, back down the stairs, exactly like the first night.

I was so tired at this point and desperate to get back to our hotel that I didn't have the energy to chase him, or fight with Krystyna again. In my defence, he hadn't asked me to keep him out on this occasion so my conscience was clear.

I was now alone, stood there on my own in a city square that was shutting down for the night. I thought that maybe Jamie would be back out in a few minutes so I hung around for a while to wait for him. A couple of lowlifes were shuffling around here and there and the area was starting to look a little eerie. After ten minutes or so and with no sign of Jamie re-appearing I thought, 'Bollocks to this, I'm off, Jamie's a big boy now.' I was completely empty and running on fumes.

I assumed I had enough zloty to be able to jump in a cab back to our hotel, so that was my plan. I crossed the road to the taxi rank and leant through the driver's window, then gave him a card with the hotel's address on it. 'Thirty zloty,' he quoted. 'I only have 20,' I said apologetically. 'Thirty zloty,' he stated again without even looking at me. 'So that's a no then?' I asked pleadingly. 'Thirty zloty!' The look was enough to end this conversation. You would think that if you are in business dealing with tourists then you would at least smile and be a little apologetic if not in a position to help someone, but no, not him. I reckon these people would be world beaters at poker as they are completely expressionless.

Now I really did have a problem. I didn't have enough cash for a taxi and I had no idea what direction to start walking even if I was brave enough. Our digs were in a proper moody part of town. There was only one thing for it so I went down the stairs into the totty bar, trying to find Jamie and hopefully get him out or at least grab ten zloty off him. As I reached the bottom of the stairs who was on the door? Krystyna. I didn't stand a chance! There was no way I was getting past this piece of work. No charm or patter of mine was going to help me this time. 'Can I just go see my mate?' I asked. 'Thirty zloty,' she barked back at me. Is every public service in this town 30 zloty? 'I only want to talk to him for a minute, I will be straight back out,' I pleaded. 'Thirty zloty,' she barked again.

She gave me a look that could kill and then said, 'I remember you trying to keep your friend away from here a couple of nights ago, now I'm in charge, so f**k you. You're not getting anywhere near your mates without paying, so unless you pay, f**k off!'

Her English was quite good. It was the look on her face that convinced me I wasn't getting in. It said, 'I win this time so go on, off you go,' and she really was so smug about it too. Sometimes in life you need to realise and accept when you're beaten. In these situations, it's best to just wipe your mouth and walk away.

I turned on my heels and was out of there. Back on the taxi rank, for a fleeting moment I truly did feel on my own, almost vulnerable. 'Stay cool,' I thought, 'keep your head together, I'll just try another taxi.' The next one that pulled up had a driver who looked big and threatening. 'Is everyone in this part of the world cast from granite?' I thought. This historically persecuted country certainly had more than its fair share of bruisers who gave the impression that they could well manage to look after Poland's interests, if history were ever to repeat itself. This guy was so big he even had muscles in his ears. I was really taking a gamble on this one – shit or bust I thought as I handed him the hotel card. 'Thirty zloty,' came his half-expected response. At least they were consistent. 'Sorry mate, I only have 20 left,' I said. 'Okay,' he mumbled and waved me in to the back of his cab.

That seemed a little too easy and my mind immediately zoomed off into overdrive. Maybe he was going to drop me off back in moody town and have some mates of his waiting to mug me. But then I had no option really, other than to wait for Jamie or any of the nutty boys coming back out of the bar. I could have been there all night.

During the week we had heard enough stories about these mugging incidents happening to some Liverpool fans. The possibility of getting mugged was real. Stories from back home emanating from newspapers and TV told of supporters getting attacked and mugged in all cities across Poland and Ukraine. Just another little issue for Donna and countless other families and loved ones to worry about. I had nothing on me to lose, I only had 20 zloty remember, but that wasn't the point. I didn't fancy a kicking. Maybe he thought I was trying to blag him and therefore he would teach me a lesson. All kinds of shite goes through your mind in situations like this, at 100 miles an hour too.

On the journey back out of town I was trying to get my bearings, trying desperately to remember landmarks we had passed on the way in. That was another old trick I learnt in my navy days travelling around the world, just to check if we appeared to be going in the right direction. It was dark and I'd had more than a couple of beers, so I had no idea. The driver said nothing, which in itself was quite a comfort as I knew he wasn't on the blower to some muscle waiting around a corner. It never ceases to amaze me how quickly you sober up in these situations but I still wouldn't have had the strength to fight back if it went off. We never did get that meal we went out for in the first place and my fuel tank was running on empty.

I was more than relieved to eventually see Wrocław's football ground swing into view. I say eventually, but in actual fact the trip had probably only taken five minutes or so. It seems an awful lot longer when you are uncertain of your ultimate destination. Sometimes, if you are unlucky, your drop-off can be very different from the one you had requested at the beginning of your journey, especially in these eastern European places that seem to have an abundance of hungry young bucks.

The taxi pulled to a stop outside my hotel. I honestly wished I'd had enough cash on me to give this bad boy a decent tip. I got to my room a very hungry but very relieved man. Lying on my bed, I started to drift away and I thought I had been there a while when I heard someone try the handle on the room door. Being half asleep and still full of beer, I thought someone was trying to break in. 'What the f**k's going on here?' I thought. I'm tired, hungry and some tosser's trying to break in, I was not a happy bunny!

I stood behind the door with a chair in my hands, above my head ready to smash it over any gobshite trying to get in to my room. I held my breath nervously as the door opened quietly. I was about to launch it when I quickly and fortunately realised it was Jamie making his way in. He had only been ten minutes or so behind me. He had only gone down into the totty bar to have a quick chat with the nutty boys after all. How he had managed to get in past Krystyna without paying was in itself a mystery to me; maybe she thought he was popping in for a dance or two and therefore ready to splash the cash. If only I had known he was right behind me, it surely would have saved me an awful lot of stress.

If I had just hung around outside the totty bar for a couple more minutes then my ride back to our hotel would have been far more enjoyable. Then again, Krystyna could have been on my case and got some of her mates over if I had waited for Jamie. You go with your gut feelings in situations like that, and maybe I had made the best call.

Jamie was telling me about the nutty boys and them throwing their cash around in the dancing bar. One of their numbers was a very young lad called Tom. He appeared to be an average sort of kid, maybe about 17 or 18 years old. All throughout our trip, every time the taxis had stopped for whatever reason, the nutty bus doors would fly open and there was Tom, seemingly totally off his tits. And I mean completely off his face. No doubt the nutty boys were looking after him, but he seemed so far out of it you couldn't help wonder if he was simply trying to keep up with, or impress the group. He seemed far too young to be playing with the big boys.

Jamie mumbled something about Tom having spent over a grand on dances. Just what sort of dance do you get for that kind of money? Heads up here Tom, you could probably have bought the bleeding club for that kind of cash. It did cross my mind however, just how does someone so young earn that kind of money to be able to throw it around in totty bars? I tried not to give it too much thought. Over-thinking things again.

26

Toilet Slaughterhouse

AFTER ANOTHER night with very little sleep, my alarm went off at 5.30am so it was a case of up, quick shower, pack and let's hit the road for the final push to Calais. At the reception, Jamie and I bumped into the Carney brothers who were checking out themselves. I was really glad to be able to say 'bon voyage' to them in person. They were both very decent lads and it was a real pleasure to have been able to get to know them. It was handshakes and hugs all round as they departed for the airport for a speedier return to Blighty as they both had work to get home for. Older brother Paul was actually in work that very same night and had a 12-hour shift to look forward to. He had to pick his car up from John Lennon Airport and then make the three-hour drive over to Lincolnshire so he could start his shift. The things we Redmen put ourselves through. The commitment, effort and expense we show over and over again never ceases to amaze me.

Occasionally, the Liverpool team have off days, just like everyone else does in any other walk of life. On those days, it can sometimes appear to us fans that the team just can't be arsed and don't really care. We can forgive defeat but will never forgive lack of effort. It was mentioned more than once by the boys on this excursion that maybe the players should be made to go on trips like this, as part of a pre-season tour. If they got to experience and understand what the fans go through to support them, maybe this would lift them in their hour of need. Who knows, they may even enjoy this type of pre-season training.

After checking out of our hotel we hit the road. Our taxi was now lighter than ever as the Carney brothers had left for the airport, as had the Bristol beauts. Jamie and I had a full bench seat each and I was determined to make this last stretch of the journey in a horizontal position, or at least a little stretched out. Spirits were still surprisingly quite high, all things considered.

We needed to refuel before we left Wrocław so we stopped at a petrol station on the outskirts of the city. As Terry fuelled up, Three Amp went inside to pay. I followed in, asking if anyone wanted a coffee or anything else. As I was making the coffees, I couldn't help notice that Jamie had followed me in and was in the anything else aisle. Unbeknown to me he was shopping again, using me as cover. 'Would that make me an accomplice?' I thought. He was right under the noses of the two petrol station attendants. Surely they could see him? They probably didn't think anyone would even try to lift anything as the place was proper secure with cameras everywhere, or maybe they didn't have the balls to pull him. Either way, the Artful Dodger was at it again. Maybe it's because he's always so calm and calculating that he never draws attention to himself and therefore he is never under suspicion. Sometimes it was jaw-dropping just watching him 'work'.

So off we went again, steaming towards the German border. A few more hours or so and we would be in the Fatherland. My consumption over the previous few days and nights, coupled with the early morning coffee, meant that it wasn't too long before my insides had started to make noises that usually require a restroom rather urgently. After what seemed an eternity and plenty of requests from me, Terry eventually managed to find somewhere to pull into. This place was signposted as a truck stop and that's all it was. Quite literally, a stop for trucks. No shops, no fuel even, nothing. It looked so uninviting.

The only things here were rows and rows of articulated lorries and nothing else but a toilet block. When I say toilet block, there was one gents' cubicle and one ladies' cubicle, although I could never imagine a lady of any description wishing to use these facilities, and one disabled cubicle, which was locked. Outside the toilets there was a small queue forming with drivers from all different parts of Europe. They were stood still in line, not saying a word to each other and all looking as miserable as sin. I was in trouble. My stomach and arse were both wanting to pay me back for the abuse they had endured over the last four days or so, with huge interest.

After waiting a while, writhing in agony, it was my turn next. Although I was desperate, I was not looking forward to this. In I went, and I froze as I opened the door. What greeted me was a sight that will live long in the memory and not in a good way. I entered the block and stood there in total shock, momentarily forgetting why I was there. I kid you not, this latrine looked like a crime scene.

Surely it should have been sealed off with that tape you see on the telly. It looked like it had been used as a slaughterhouse, similar to a scene straight out of *The Texas Chain Saw Massacre*. What had gone on in here, I just couldn't begin to comprehend.

There was so much blood everywhere; on the walls, on the floor, even on the ceiling. My mind was racing, imagining all sorts of scenarios. I composed myself and tried desperately to block these thoughts from my head as I went inside the cubicle. Conditions didn't improve on the inside either; no toilet seat, not even a lock on the door. A man's got to do what a man's got to do so I had no alternative but to go for it. Maybe I was too traumatised to notice at first but I hadn't even clocked the fact that there was no toilet paper. Why was I surprised? Shorts back up, I crabbed my way back to our taxi. I literally had to crab, because any more of a strenuous movement could have easily spelt disaster. Sweating profusely as I desperately held on, I made it back to the lads. 'Any wet wipes left boys?' Bless them servicemen once again.

I was soon back in the queue awaiting my turn once again. I eventually made it in, blinkered this time, and made my way in to the cubicle. There, I was squatting as there was no way on earth my skin was touching anything at all in this hell hole. Knees trembling, body shaking and still sweating, believe me when I say the job was quickly completed. No playing on phones or reading the *Echo*!

I ever so cautiously made my way back towards the taxi and the lads, who were waiting patiently for me. I swear

I was still sweating and shaking when I opened the door. I was looking like a man well beaten by such a traumatic experience. The boys were silent and just sat there looking at me. I couldn't make out whether it was a sympathetic look or a congratulatory one. Eventually, though, I started to feel a little better and recompose myself so the taxi was off once again.

A little bit further up the road, Three Amp suggested breakfast so we could get rid of the last of any Polish zloty before we crossed the border into Germany. I couldn't believe my ears when I heard Three Amp say that we should stop for a break. This was the same man who had moaned and snarled at almost every stop we had taken since leaving Liverpool.

It was a little before 8am when Terry pulled into yet another service area. I honestly didn't think I could handle any more fast food so I declined the offer of a Burger King breakfast. Outside the cafe was a big billboard showing what was on offer and the price list. 'Right,' said Jamie, 'I've still got enough of this Monopoly money for a burger, anyone coming over?' Three Amp accompanied Jamie into the cafe and for some reason Terry shot off in the opposite direction. I stayed behind and sat on a picnic table at the side of the taxi. I was thoroughly enjoying yet another beautiful early summer's morning waiting for the boys to return. Three Amp was first to come back. 'That Burger King place isn't open yet,' he said as he mooched off in the same direction Terry had gone in minutes earlier. Shortly after Three Amp had followed Terry, Jamie returned with not one but two burgers in hand. Firstly the place was closed, and secondly he just about had enough cash for one burger. Yet there he was, with one in each hand.

'You may as well have one of these, Steve,' he said. 'I don't fancy two.' True enough, they were whoppers! I reluctantly accepted his offer, proclaiming that this was definitely the last burger that would ever pass my lips, not just on this trip but for the rest of my life.

I had long gone past the objective of trying to work out how Jamie managed to get things done. This boy could make the impossible, possible. A talent?

27

Deathbahns

WE SET off once more and finally rolled across the border into Germany at about 10am. The terrain had changed dramatically as we left behind the rolling fields of Poland. As soon as we hit eastern Germany, all that we could see for miles was large coal pits and big slag heaps. This part of Germany looked completely deserted. The pits seemed to go on for eternity but nothing appeared to be moving in or around them so we assumed they must have been closed down. One of the boys joked, 'Maybe Maggie Thatcher was here as well!' What a funny but thought-provoking comment that was.

It is common knowledge that the Germans have no speed limit on their autobahns. Although there are calls back home to increase the limits on our motorways, I wouldn't be in favour of this. Some of the scenes we witnessed on these German roads were so horrific that they made me certain of my belief.

We caught the aftermath of three prangs on these race circuits. No one, and I do mean no one, was walking away from these accidents. All three incidents involved high-performance cars. We guessed that one was a Porsche, one a Ferrari and none of us could even manage a guess as to the make of the third one, because of the state it was in. It looked as though it had been through a crusher. The drivers of the cars may have been rich, successful and living a very nice life but not one of these people would be going home. There was no way on earth anybody could have survived such carnage. Give me the old 70 miles an hour speed limit at home any day. Why on earth are motoring manufacturers allowed to make cars that go so fast, especially for use on public roads? Madness in my humble opinion, for what that's worth.

As we made progress along the autobahn, Three Amp was getting a little excited. He had noticed on the sat nav that we weren't too far from a famous European football stadium. 'Boys, Dortmund's ground isn't too far away, anyone fancy calling in to see it?' he asked with great enthusiasm. A cue for plenty of Everton jokes again but all were in agreement.

Terry reset the sat nav for the Westfalenstadion, the home of Borussia Dortmund, Jürgen Klopp's old stomping ground. Three Amp was really quite excited and even ignored the jokes about blue boys never getting to see big-time European grounds.

As we took the slip road towards Dortmund and their stadium, it was requested that we should stop to have another quick toilet break. The first petrol station we came to was just around the corner from the ground. As we pulled in, we could see the official Borussia Dortmund team bus parked up. Three Amp was chuffed to bits to see it, bless him. As our taxi pulled to a halt, Jamie said to Terry, 'Go round again and pull up on the other side of the Dortmund bus this time.'

'Why do we need to do that?' asked Terry. 'Just go round again, the door on their bus is open and there's no f****r about,' replied Jamie enthusiastically. 'Jay, why do we need to do that?' Terry asked again. 'I've just clocked a Dortmund shirt on it and it might belong to one of their players and my lad would be made up with that.' 'Jay, it's not like we are going straight back on the motorway and getting off sharp, is it?' I butted in with my sensible head on. 'What do you mean?' he asked. 'We're going about 200 yards around the corner to their ground, the German plod will be all over us within minutes,' I reasoned. 'Won't be a problem, we can do it,' he almost begged. 'No chance Jay,' came the stern answer from Terry. 'Shower of c***s,' he mumbled in defeat. To be fair to Jamie, I think he could understand the logic and never really put up much of a fight. We did get a photo stood next to the bus though.

We drove around to the ground, climbed out of our taxi, took a couple of photos, and we were off again. It was hardly worth the detour, especially as I had been there before, but Three Amp was happy enough.

I have much better memories of my last visit to this stadium. Back in 2001 I took Donna and one of our daughters, Leanne, there, to watch the UEFA Cup Final. That was a trip to remember. On that particular jolly we had decided to fly into Amsterdam, have a night there and then catch a train down to Dortmund the next morning, the day of the game.

Anyone in Amsterdam that night would have sworn that they were back home in Liverpool on New Year's Eve. An estimated 12,000 Reds supporters were there on the eve of the final, a truly amazing street party. Why wouldn't anyone want to do it?

On the morning of the game itself, Amsterdam Central resembled Lime Street Station on FA Cup Final day back home. From the early hours, train after train heading into Germany was full of Redmen on the march.

Liverpool won the old UEFA Cup that night in Dortmund after yet another incredible game, against Alavés from Spain. The final finished 5-4 to us in extra time, as we won the cup on the now abandoned golden goal rule. Next goal wins basically – the rule we often used as kids on the corner of the street.

It's a rule that I think we should still adopt in the game today. Survival of the fittest and all that, and surely a much fairer way of settling a match rather than the lottery of a penalty shoot-out. It certainly was a trip to remember but maybe I will keep that story for another day.

After our brief stop at the stadium, we were back on the road heading west. Although we were making good ground, we still had another three borders to cross, excluding the ferry crossing back to our little island.

The rest of Germany passed by without much happening, as did most of Holland. I think fatigue was kicking in for most of us.

28

Handtwerp

OUR SHORT drive through Belgium was more one of short shunts because our timing couldn't have been much worse. We happened to hit the old city of Antwerp at rush hour. Trying to navigate your way through a major city at this time of day can be slow and painful in any country. Antwerp was no different, but this leg of the trip wasn't painful at all, it was unexpectedly entertaining.

We edged through Belgium's second largest city at no more than crawling pace. Stop-start with all of the other cars, vans and HGVs filling the lanes to bursting point, all heading in the same direction. We were on a motorway in the middle of a city centre so as you can imagine, it really was gridlocked.

Jamie was talking to his beloved on his phone when he suddenly said to her, 'Hang on babe, call you back in a minute.' Even before he had pressed the end call button, he turned to us and said, 'F****n' hell, he's f****n' her there!' 'What, where?' was the disbelieving reply from the rest of us. 'Over there on the left, in that red car,' he said, laughingly.

All eyes turned left and there it was, this red motor shunting alongside us in the inside lane. The driver, like us, was crawling along in his rather average car on a rather average day. What was going on inside the vehicle could only be described as completely not average at all. This fella was really 'feeding the horse', to quote Keith Lemon, the comedian. In early evening rush hour in the middle of Antwerp! Crawling along an inner-city ring road at the busiest time of the day. The things some people will do to relieve their boredom. His travelling companion was a young, good-looking woman of maybe mid-to-late 20s and she was in heaven, or at least she certainly gave the impression she was. The boys were transfixed.

I swear that if any one of us were alone in witnessing this event and attempted to relay the story to others, the cries of 'bullshit!' would be deafening. I kid you not though, this was happening. What's more, his female companion was absolutely loving it and was displaying plenty of enthusiasm. He certainly knew how to please her.

This entertainment carried on for more than a few minutes as our taxi and their car kept swapping positions in the snail race to get through the city centre. The fella in the car was soon on to the fact that they had an audience. Did this stop him, did he tell the woman, who had her eyes closed? No, he just gave a thumbs-up to his audience and in the words of the song by The Beautiful South, just 'carried on regardless'. What a bloke, pleasing a woman, giving a thumbs-up and driving his car all at the same time. What a talent, credit where it's due. Multi-tasking at its best!

As all good things do, this had to come to an end. This young woman got to whereever she was going and collapsed back into her passenger seat, with a big smile on her face. It was then that Jamie piped up with a classic, 'Did anyone notice she wasn't wearing a seat belt?' There's humour to be found in most scenarios.

At this point the traffic was standing still. After such a show, it was suggested that surely some sign of appreciation was in order. The side door to our taxi was swung open. I stepped out in to the stationary motorway traffic and proceeded to lead the round of applause we all thought was due.

This was the moment the young lady must have realised that her little pleasure trip had captured an audience and she quickly came to her senses. Both hands came up to hide her face as a bright red colour overcame her. The fella obviously didn't feel quite as embarrassed as a huge smile and double thumbs were sent in our direction. Her embarrassment hadn't quite finished. As our taxi edged forward, offers of wet wipes and toilet rolls were being held out of our windows as we passed each other one last time.

I struggled to understand her embarrassment; she knew and quite obviously enjoyed what she was doing! This lovely lady must have suggested to the man that she'd had enough attention for one day, as within minutes their car started weaving through the crawling traffic in an effort to shake off their new-found fans.

As their car disappeared into the distance, Three Amp was straight on the phone to his girl back home, 'Hey babe, you okay?' Before giving her a chance to reply, he went on, 'You won't believe what we've all just seen. You know that thing I've been asking you to do for ages in the car? I swear down we've all just seen it. Honestly babe, they were proper goin' for it.'

Three Amp seemed so sincere that he almost made it sound such a natural thing to do and couldn't understand why his beloved hadn't conformed in the past, especially now, after witnessing it first-hand himself. I'm certain he was trying to convince her it was only natural and everyone does it. It was so funny to listen to a one-sided conversation of this context; it didn't take much imagination to guess what was being said on the other end of the line though.

After we had finally got through Antwerp on our way to the French border, Three Amp was banging on about how good Gent's ground had looked a few days earlier. None of us had seen the stadium on the way in as most of us were sound asleep. This was mainly due to the unearthly hour that we had passed through Belgium on the Wednesday morning. We were all scanning the landscape with anticipation, all except Jamie that is, who was on the phone to his missus and kids, again. When the stadium came into view, although nice and new, it looked more like Brighton than the Bernabéu. Maybe Three Amp was excited but the rest of us had been lucky enough to have seen bigger and better on our travels.

We were hours ahead of the rest of the convoy and making great strides even though we had been slightly delayed in Belgium. I can honestly say I didn't hear one single complaint in reference to our little traffic jam, not even from Three Amp. For obvious reasons this Belgian city will now be forever known as Handtwerp to the unfortunate boys who were forced to witness this exhibition.

29

Homeward-Bound

WE LEFT Belgium behind, steaming ahead for northern France, when our Terry decided to check in with Terry the owner and get some details for the ferry crossing. He came off the phone. 'Boys,' he said. 'I've just been told that we're a bit early for the ferry we are booked on.' 'Sound, what time are we supposed to be on the boat?' I asked. 'At five. In the morning,' came the hesitant reply. We were ten hours early!

'Well, we'll just have to drive up and blag it,' said Three Amp. What happened next left the rest of us completely stunned and gobsmacked once again. Totally out of the blue and rather bizarrely, Jamie went into acting mode. Unusually, he was actually sat up front in the passenger seat opposite Terry, when he suddenly started to turn on the waterworks. Bottom lip going, sobbing gently through his words, he turned it on; this bloke was a pro. Although none of us had seen this side of his character, he was rather impressive. 'What's all that about, Jamie?' enquired Three Amp. 'If we need to blag it, I'm goin' for the sympathy vote,' he said. 'I'll tell 'em me ma or da's just died, they might let us get on an earlier boat.'

As it happened, none of his amateur dramatics were required but fair play to him for using his initiative. I wondered how many times his acting skills had got him out of tricky situations in the past.

We rolled up to the checkpoint in Calais, where the French lady booking the vehicles on to the ferry took one look at us sat in our taxi and said, 'This is the DFDS ferry port, you need the P&O port.' P&O were on the other side of town. It was a little after 7pm and we knew there was an 8pm sailing from the correct terminal, if we could make it.

We had been lucky in the way our trip had panned out so far and with Terry's new-found expertise in driving on European roads, I for one was confident we could make it. Twenty minutes later and we were in line, edging towards the correct terminal this time. Jamie was preparing to get in character just in case.

No one had given too much thought to the fact that we had a few extra cartons of cigarettes on board, not to mention the three sets of kitchen knives we had acquired back in Poland. This was on top of other gifts that were now taking up a considerable amount of the luggage space in our taxi.

We reached the ferry check-in booth and handed in our passports. We were all hoping that they would let us on the earlier ferry. If need be, we were even willing to hand over the goodies on board, pay an admin charge or whatever it took, without question, just to get on the next ferry. Passports in, the mademoiselle took a quick look into our bus. Without leaving her seat in what resembled one of those booths you go through at the Birkenhead side of the Mersey Tunnels back home, she said, 'Paul.' 'Here,' he replied. 'Jamie.' 'Here.' 'Stephen.' 'Here.' 'Terry.' 'Here.'

That was it, we got our passports back and we were through. No mention whatsoever of the fact that we were attempting to get on a ferry nine hours before our booking. It was great news for us but once again alarming to say the least. The border controls on both sides of the Channel were pathetically slack, and in saying that, I really am being kind. To be honest, if it weren't for the accent, I would have sworn it was the same border agency that had let us leave England with ease a few days earlier.

We could quite easily have brought back one or more of those people who had wandered out from the infamous 'jungle' at Calais. We had passed many of these along the way and it certainly appeared an easy thing to accomplish. It's frightening, when you stop to think about it.

Once on board the ferry, Jamie was straight on his phone again. After one of his conversations he stopped to relay to us that the nutty bus had encountered even more mechanical problems since they had left Ukraine and things got worse as they limped through Poland. On the other hand, owner Terry, who was driving the Bible bus, had made good progress and was well on his way through Germany heading for home. Well out of the reach of the nutty bus, which had actually left our hotel in Wrocław about six hours after the rest of us had departed. I presumed that was because they couldn't get out of their beds after such a heavy night.

Jamie remarked that being so far ahead was very lucky for Terry. My immediate thought was that Terry was in big shit when they caught up with him back on home soil. Another comment or two from Jamie confirmed this.

Remember that Jamie knew these bad boys from back home, and they were not the sort to let things go. These fellas were serious naughty boys and once you upset these people, you would pay for it one way or the other. Jamie mentioned that a sincere apology was usually enough to make this problem go away. With no apology so far and none seemingly on the horizon, I thought this could get nasty. These troops wouldn't stay wronged for long; they had a lot of face to save and the last thing they ever worried about was the consequences of their actions.

A couple of days after our return, Jamie told me the rest of the story. The final straw was when their taxi had come to a standstill on the autobahn not too far from Dortmund. This transpired to be a fuel problem, or lack of it, as they would soon find out. Before this revelation though, it was assumed it was yet another breakdown and to make matters worse, Terry wasn't returning their calls.

One of its occupants was so enraged that he immediately made a phone call back home. The call was to order a hit on owner Terry's company office! Luckily for all involved the fuel issue was quickly resolved and the attack was called off. The hitmen were actually en route when they received the call to abort.

I feel I must add again that these troops are no problem to anyone if you let them be and leave them to play in their own little world. Interfere or do them wrong and you will probably live to regret it.

We finally docked at the port of Dover at around 8pm on the Tuesday. Although the return ferry from Calais was a quieter affair, the boat was still full of Scousers. I managed to catch up with a fella from work who had also gone on another mammoth road trip from The Arkles. Michael Tremarco is an old-school scally but another very decent bloke. He is more mature and subdued now but would still do anything for you. His trip was on a luxury coach that left about two hours after our convoy had pulled away on that same Tuesday evening. Our taxis and his coach had crossed paths on a few occasions during the trip but we hadn't actually caught up with each other.

We finally got to enjoy a beer together in the bar on the ferry home and reflected on yet another wonderful experience. Michael was sat with his mate Barry Rimmer, who I also knew. Along with Donna, we had all recently been on a trip together to the eternal city of Rome, via Switzerland, having been to watch the Reds play AS Roma in the semi-final second leg of this year's Champions League. That was another fabulous trip mixing the football with a bit of culture at the same time.

I know I keep saying it but these European away trips really are something else. If ever you find yourself with even the slightest chance to go on one, then I urge you to grab it with both hands and squeeze it very tight. Milk it for everything it's worth and then enjoy the memories. A home game is good, a domestic away game is better, and an away European match is just off the scale.

As the three of us reminisced about this and previous trips, I was glancing around as we chatted. You couldn't help notice that the few previous days' excitement was starting to show and plenty of the troops were flagging. The ferry home, although not silent, was a little quieter. Our convoy had long since broken up so exactly which taxi was on which boat was anyone's guess.

Back in Blighty it was going to be one long slog back to Liverpool with the only planned stops being to refuel. Terry was truly knackered by this point, so the final leg was left to Three Amp. Earlier I had offered my services to help with the driving as I could see how tired both drivers were and wanted to help if I could, but I wasn't insured. Jamie was also wiped out so it was left to me to keep Three Amp entertained, and more importantly help him stay awake on this last shunt home. Fair play to the big man, he didn't need much help as he did most of the talking. We eventually returned to the people's republic of Merseyside a full 152 hours after departing. There were big handshakes and hugs all round when Jamie turned and said to me, 'Ste, would you do it again?' 'In a heartbeat,' was my instant reply. 'Even with the same result?' he asked. 'Yeah, in a heartbeat mate,' I said again.

This experience of our little adventure across Europe will stay with me forever. It started out with a group of strangers from all different backgrounds who, over the course of six days bonded and became mates, who you know would always watch your back and be there for you if the need ever arose.

Our paths may not have been destined to cross for months, years or even possibly ever again. But one thing was for certain – if we were ever to meet again, then a nod, a wink or a handshake would be all that it would take.

30

Merseyside United

AS THERE have been a few references in this book to Reds and Blues, I felt I could not finish without expressing my personal memories and thoughts on this, our world-famous relationship.

The Merseyside cup finals back in the 1980s were a blast. I only got to experience these finals with my younger brother Tony as Paul, my elder sibling, was married with a young family, and his priorities rightly lay elsewhere. He ended up with two boys and a wife who are all Reds, so I'd call that a real result.

These days Paul tends to run with the fox and the hounds. He is blue underneath but will watch whoever dangles the biggest carrot. His eldest boy, also called Paul, is employed in an industry that uses corporate hospitality to wine and dine its employees and clients at various sporting venues. My brother and his good lady Les are often invited to piggy-back in to some of these events. Paul has never been one to turn down a free lunch no matter where it is being offered. He has on more than one occasion sat among the Mancs at Old Trafford, enjoying his champagne and caviar, to his eternal shame!

Back in the day all Scousers stuck together, whether they were Reds or Blues. We were united and partied together, long and hard. I remember the Merseyside United trip down to Wembley in 1986, or Anfield South as it was known back then. The London plod couldn't believe their eyes.

I remember having one particular conversation with a member of the Met Police as soon as I had stepped off the train at Euston Station on the Friday morning. He told me that all police leave had been cancelled in the capital for that weekend. Trouble was anticipated as they were expecting 150,000 Scousers to invade their manor. Their numbers weren't far wrong but the expected trouble was never going to happen, not in those days. Their time would have been spent more wisely watching jewellery shops and sports clothing establishments in the greater London area rather than looking out for football hooligans.

Coincidentally, I bumped into the very same policeman on my return to Euston on the Sunday evening on my way home. The station was awash with young bucks all sleeping together under red and blue flags. This copper and his colleagues were in awe; the things they had observed over this weekend were so far removed from the anticipated troubles his seniors and their intel had predicted. He told me that he had never witnessed anything like it: two big rival sets of football supporters all singing, dancing and partying together, for a whole weekend. He was also happy to mention that his overtime had never been so easily earned. It's so sad, but it looks as though those days will never return. The 1980s were the peak of this unique relationship.

The Heysel Stadium Disaster in Brussels on 29 May 1985 was the start of the end, or should I say the consequences of that horrendous night were. The loss of life at any age in any circumstances is painful enough, but for 39 poor souls to have perished at a football match is completely incomprehensible. I was in that stadium on that fateful night. So-called Liverpool supporters were very much at the centre of things but were never the entirely guilty party that they were portrayed to be.

Many incidents had preceded that ultimate surge across the terracing that evening. Liverpool fans had been getting picked off at random by gangs of Italians parading around the streets of Brussels not only on the day of the game but on the evening before too. Two wrongs don't make a right and indeed UEFA had an awful lot to answer for themselves. It was without doubt the worst kept and least secure stadium I had ever entered in my life. I was in a party of 57 people and if I am correct, I think over 50 of us had entered the stadium without our tickets getting checked once that night. That in itself was a disaster waiting to happen.

The European ban that followed robbed that year's title-winning Everton team of the chance to compete at the very highest level the following season. This was a team that was great to watch, possibly up there with Everton's greatest ever, and packed with international players of the very highest calibre. The consequences of Heysel forced the club to sell quite a few of their top players. Quite understandably these boys were desperate to play in Europe's top competitions so they were off, leaving a very unsettled team behind.

English clubs were banned for five years and as the protagonists, Liverpool received a further one-year ban.

Everton were never to reach those dizzy heights ever again and as such our unique relationship started to deteriorate and unfortunately will never recover.

Strangely, that ban only applied to English club teams, yet the marauding hordes following the England national team across Europe and beyond were left to carry on.

Some say this unwittingly encouraged certain club hooligans who were banned from following their own clubs to start following England.

Maggie Thatcher had called for the ban to begin with. Those of us old enough to remember will never forget the chaos and damage caused by England fans at the Italian World Cup in 1990, during the domestic club ban. The irony!

Back in the day, it was far from uncommon to see both Reds and Blues attending each other's games together, all having a laugh and on the make. If I am being completely honest, I probably enjoyed going to Goodison Park more than going to Anfield, simply because I didn't care what the result was. It was just a good day out with my brothers or mates, and usually both.

I rarely missed any of the Liverpool or Everton home games back in the early 1980s. If a big match was on the horizon with either club then it was quite common to see the boys from both teams running together, home and away. You would also often see some of the Blues roaming across Europe with the Redmen, enjoying what the continent had to offer.

It is with huge regret and sadness that I have to say that the Merseyside derbies have turned a little sinister these days. The younger generation have taken it upon themselves to spread hatred and venom. This confuses me on a rather large scale. Their new-found attitude can only ever have been passed down from their forefathers, yet there never appeared to be any bother at all between our generation in days gone by. I scratch my head.

The Heysel ban was the catalyst for our relationship's demise but almost four decades on, the poison that is now spat in both directions carries so much more venom than at any time since the disaster in 1985. We all have our own ideas and reasons as to how this has come to be.

Both parties are culpable but now it appears to have gone to extremes. Some are more guilty than others no doubt but weren't we once the envy of England, Europe and indeed the rest of the world for our tremendous derby day relationship?

So much has my relationship with Everton fans deteriorated that I have not been anywhere near Goodison Park since 2001, and nor will I ever again. It was the anniversary weekend of the Hillsborough disaster and more than one incident involving their fans turned my stomach that afternoon. It got to the point where I couldn't stay in the stadium any longer, so moments before that famous Gary McAllister winner, I left the stadium and vowed never to return. I'm sure there are Blues who feel the same way about visiting Anfield. Sadly, I would say our offspring and our future generations are the losers in this one. Us Red and Blue forefathers had some amazing times together, on the run, having fun and making some. Yet we have so much to answer for today.

Acknowledgements

A HUGE thank you to my beloved wife Donna, who was the one who gave me the belief and the encouragement to persevere with this project, and not to mention the countless English lessons. In fact, she arranged for me to go to Kyiv in the first place. Donna is constant support in everything I have attempted during our time together.

A big thank you not only to the boys who travelled in our taxi and gave me something to write about, but also to the thousands of Redmen and women who made the long trip into Ukraine.

Another top trip and another huge success, off the pitch anyway.

One of the great things about following Liverpool FC around is that there's always another trip to look forward to, another 'next time'.

The completion of this book couldn't have come at a more perfect time. After I closed my laptop I headed off to pack for Madrid but this time Donna was coming with me for the 2019 Champions League Final. We boxed clever for this one and booked our flights before the semi-final against Barcelona.

For once, it came up trumps!

Y.N.W.A.

RIP 97